C PROGRAMMING GUIDE

Jack Purdum

Que Corporation
Indianapolis

Cover art: Louie LeVier
Artwork: Dennis Sheehan
Design: Paul Mangin
Typeset in Helvetica by Alexander Typesetting, Inc.

Manufactured in the United States of America

Published by Que Corporation
7960 Castleway Drive
Indianapolis, Indiana 46250

About the Author

Jack Purdum

Dr. Purdum received his B.A. degree from Muskingum College and M.A. and Ph.D. degrees from Ohio State University. He is currently Associate Professor of Economics at Butler University where he teaches both computer programming and economics courses. Dr. Purdum has received many teaching and research awards, including a National Science Foundation grant to study microcomputers in education. He has published a number of professional articles; a BASIC programming text, and magazine articles in *Byte, Personal Computing* and *Interface Age.* Dr. Purdum is president of Ecosoft, a software house that specializes in microcomputer software.

Editorial Director
David F. Noble, Ph.D.

Editor
Diane F. Brown, M.A.

Managing Editor
Paul L. Mangin

Assistant Managing Editor
Tim P. Russell

Technical Editor
Chris DeVoney

Technical Advisor
Steve Browning

Dedication

to my family:
Karol, Katie, and John Paul

Que Microcomputer Products

BOOKS:	ISBN No.	Date Available
Apple II Word Processing	0-88022-005-8	Currently
C Programming Guide	0-88022-022-8	Spring, '83
CP/M Compatible Software Catalog 2nd Ed.	0-88022-018-X	Currently
CP/M Word Processing	0-88022-006-6	Currently
IBM PC Expansion & Software Guide	0-88022-019-8	Currently
IBM PC Pocket Dictionary	0-88022-024-4	Spring, '83
IBM's Personal Computer-hbk.	0-88022-101-1	Currently
IBM's Personal Computer-pbk.	0-88022-100-3	Currently
The Osborne Portable Computer	0-88022-015-5	Currently
Personal Computers for Managers	0-88022-031-7	May, '83
SuperCalc SuperModels for Business	0-88022-007-4	
Timex/Sinclair 1000 User's Guide, Vol. 1	0-88022-016-3	Currently
Timex/Sinclair 1000 User's Guide, Vol. 2	0-88022-029-5	Currently
Timex/Sinclair 1000 Pocket Dictionary	0-88022-028-7	Spring, '83
VisiCalc Models for Business	0-88022-017-1	March, '83

SOFTWARE:

CalcSheets for Business	1100 Series	Currently

"CalcSheets for Business" is a series of VisiCalc and SuperCalc models to assist businesspeople in cash management, debt management, fixed asset management, working capital management, and other business management. These models run on the IBM Personal Computer, Apple II computer and other popular personal computers.

Table of Contents

Preface

This text is designed to teach you how to write programs in the C language. The fact that you are reading this preface suggests that you already know some of the advantages C has over other languages. With its extensive set of operators and data types, C is a very flexible language that lets you write anything from operating systems to accounting packages. The many other advantages will become clear as you read this text.

The book was written with two underlying assumptions: (1) the only way to learn a language is to write programs with it, and (2) learning is made easier if you can visualize what a program statement does. This text explains in an easy-to-read manner how to use C and why. Several appendixes explore certain topics in greater depth for the interested reader.

Each chapter contains program examples that introduce additional elements of the C language. Each program is kept as simple as possible, but still conveys the topic at hand. The text encourages you to experiment with each program. Sometimes questions are asked that can be answered only if you run the program. In this sense, the text may be used as a self-study guide. In a formal classroom setting, these questions can be used for lab projects to reinforce the content of the chapter.

To build on previous knowledge, the book occasionally presents side-by-side comparisons with the BASIC programming language. This strategy makes the transition to C easier for those who have worked with BASIC. Even if you do not know a programming language, you can learn C. Simple graphic representations are also used so that you can ''see'' what a particular instruction does. This is particularly helpful if you do not already know a programming language.

We have also tried to minimize the cost to you of experimenting with C. All the program examples in the first five chapters can be run with C compilers that are priced under $50. (Many of the program examples in subsequent chapters can also be run with these compilers.) By the time you read the later chapters, you should be convinced of the virtues of C and will probably want to invest in a full C compiler.

This book was a joint effort; many individuals contributed to the final product. In particular, I would like to thank Steve Browning and Chris DeVoney for their suggestions and critical attention to detail; Tim Leslie, who can always find one more detail to criticize; the publisher and editorial staff at Que, who don't know what a 40-hour week is; and finally, Ron Cain for his public-domain C compiler that has done so much to popularize C.

Foreword

The programs and functions in this book were tested on several different C compilers running under the CP/M operating system. Most programs and examples will run on any C compiler that is UNIX-version-7 compatible. Less sophisticated compilers may also be used. Some programs in the later chapters (6 through 9) involve floating-point variables; these may not be available on less sophisticated compilers.

Because the implementation of C's standard library varies between compiler publishers, you should review your documentation for any peculiarities, differences in function calls, or additional program lines that should be added to the program examples for your compiler. One example is the inclusion of `stdio.h`. Some compilers demand that this file be included with every program file, while others require this file for only specific operations, such as reading and writing disk files. (The `stdio.h` file is covered in Chapters 5 and 8.)

To increase legibility, the programs, examples, C keywords, and variables are set in a font called OCR-B. This font is reproduced below.

```
ABCDEFGHIJKLMNOPQRSTUVWXYZ
abcdefghijklmnopqrstuvwxyz
0123456789
!"#$%&'()*+,-./
:;<=>?@[]\^_{|}~
```

A ruler line is provided below to help you count the spaces in a program line.

```
    0    1    1    2    2    3    3    4    4    5    5    6
1234567890123456789012345678901234567890123456789012345678901234567890123456789012
```

Chapter 1
An Introduction to C

This text is designed to help you learn to write programs in C as quickly as possible. To this end, simple examples are used to illustrate each aspect of the C language. Many of these examples can be run using inexpensive C compilers. Therefore, you need not invest much money if you are just "investigating" C at this point.

It is helpful, however, if you have access to a C compiler as you read this text. Appendix B lists several moderately priced C compilers. Even if you use the least expensive one on the list (less than $20.00), you will be able to run all of the programs in the first five chapters of this text. Some programs in later chapters require a full-featured C compiler, but you should find C worth the investment by then.

Why C?

C has many advantages over other programming languages. It is a robust language whose large variety of operators and commands can be used to write anything from operating systems to accounting packages. In fact, many of the C compilers on the market today were written in C.

C is a portable language. A C program written on one computer can be run with little or no modification on any other computer with a C compiler. The idea of "write it once" takes on real meaning with C.

Another advantage is C's execution speed. If you have never worked with a compiler and are accustomed to using an interpreted language such as BASIC, you're in for a pleasant surprise. For example, one program in Chapter 2 does nothing more than increment a variable from 0 to 30,000. In a totally unfair test, the interpreted BASIC version took 96 seconds, but the C version took less than 2 seconds.

The advantages of portability and speed combine to form another subtle advantage. Situations arise where execution speed is critical; sorting is a common example. Coding the program in assembly language was the usual solution. The problem was that, as new Central Processing Unit (CPU) chips were introduced, the programmer was forced to learn a new instruction set for each CPU. Retraining costs were so high that many commercial software houses (including a major supplier of BASIC interpreters) switched to C for in-house development.

This logic also applies to you. Although you will have to spend some time to learn C, you won't have to waste time learning a new language each time a new CPU comes on the market. With a good C compiler, the difference in execution speed between C and an assembler will go unnoticed in all but the most demanding cases.

Another advantage is that C lends itself well to structured programming techniques, forcing you to think of function modules or *blocks*. Each block has a specialized purpose or *function*. A C program involves little more than arranging these modules to perform the overall task of the program. This modular approach makes program debugging and maintenance easier.

Finally, C is an enjoyable language—not necessarily because it's easy to learn, but because it's flexible. By creating your own function modules, you can make C do just about anything you want. If you are so inclined, you can create your own language in C! Before you set off in that direction, however, let's press on with the task at hand: learning C.

Some Assumptions about the Reader

This text makes several assumptions about you—the first one being that you have access to a computer, a text editor (for entering the programs into the computer and saving them on disk), and a C compiler. The exact compiler doesn't matter at this point. The important thing is to try the examples *as they are presented in the text*. You cannot learn a language by reading about it; you have to plunge right in.

The second assumption is that you are familiar with some elements of programming, and the BASIC programming language in particular. This assumption should *not* be viewed as prohibitive. Even if you do not know a programming language, you should be able to learn C. However, "side-by-side" versions of a program or routine in C and the corresponding one in BASIC are used as a learning tool in this text. BASIC is used to build on any programming knowledge you may have.

The last assumption is that there is no pressure on you to master C by tomorrow evening. Some chapters may dwell on a point longer than you think is necessary. This approach is used because C is a pyramid that must rest on a solid foundation. Take the time to master the contents of a chapter before proceeding to the next one. Working each example is a step in the right direction. It is also important to experiment and enjoy yourself while you're learning. Understanding what is written in this text is not the same as writing your own programs.

Fundamental Characteristics of C Programs

Functions in C

All C programs can be viewed as a group of building blocks called *functions. A function is a group of one or more C statements designed to accomplish a specific task*. Study the programs in Figure 1.1.

Figure 1.1

```
/*                      C                      */
/* this C program prints a message on the screen */
main()
{
     printf("This is my first program.\n");

}
```

```
10 REM This BASIC program does the same thing
20 PRINT "This is my first program."
30 END
```

This program is written first in C and then in BASIC. Both versions print the message: This is my first program. In C, a program *comment* or *remark* begins with a forward-slash asterisk combination (**/***) and ends with the two characters reversed (***/**). Everything between these marks is ignored by the C compiler. The comment serves the same purpose as the REM (i.e., REMark) statement in BASIC. Both are nonexecuting program statements.

Hint: Because the compiler ignores everything between **/*** and ***/**, these comment characters can be a useful debugging tool. If you want to remove a line from a C program for testing, surrounding it by comment characters will have the same effect. You can remove an entire program section this way without having to type it back in later. When the comment characters are removed, the "commented-out" line is restored.

The main() Function

The special function **main()** marks the point where a C program begins execution. Every program *must* have a **main()** function to show the compiler where the program starts. This function can be used only once in a program. If several **main()** functions were used, the compiler could not tell which **main()** marked the start of the program.

Throughout this text, any reference to a function name has opening and closing parentheses immediately after it to help you recognize the name as a function. For example, the parentheses help you distinguish the function named **main()** from the word *main*.

Braces

The *opening brace ({)*, directly below the letter **m** in **main()** in Figure 1.1, *marks the beginning of the function body*. The *function body* contains one or more program statements that are used to perform a specific task.

Ignoring what **printf()** is for the moment, you can see a closing brace (}) at the bottom of the C program. This brace *marks the end of the function body*. The opening and closing braces, therefore, "surround" the statement(s) that form the function body. Figure 1.2 highlights what we have covered so far. Dots are used to represent statement(s) within the function body.

Figure 1.2

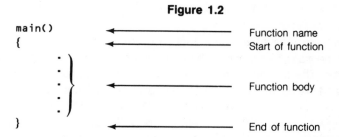

```
main()                 ◀───────────────────   Function name
{                      ◀───────────────────   Start of function

   . ⎫
   . ⎬                 ◀───────────────────   Function body
   . ⎭

}                      ◀───────────────────   End of function
```

The closing brace serves another purpose when it is used with **main()**. Just as the opening brace of **main()** marks the beginning of a C program, *the closing brace of* **main()** *marks the end of the program*.

Determining where a BASIC programs starts execution is easy; it begins with the lowest line number in the program. Unless told to do otherwise, BASIC processes the program by ascending line numbers until it finds an END statement. The END statement in line 30 of Figure 1.1 causes the program to terminate.

Because C programs do not use line numbers, the opening and closing braces for the **main()** function are used to mark the beginning and end of a program even when other C statements follow the closing brace in **main()**.

To reinforce this idea, let's suppose that we could write a "BASIC-like" C program similar to the programs in Figure 1.1. This new program is shown in Figure 1.3.

Figure 1.3

```
main()     /* this is a phony BASIC-like C program */
{

    X$ = "This is my first program.\n";
    GOSUB printf(X$);

}
END

printf(X$)     /* a call to a function */
{

    PRINT X$;
    RETURN;

}
```

If this program behaved like an actual program, it would begin execution with the **main()** function. The function body of **main()** has two statements. The first statement assigns a string of characters to **X$**. The second statement is a GOSUB that calls another function named **printf()**, which prints the contents of **X$**. The RETURN statement in **printf()** sends control back to **main()** for further processing. Because there are no further statements in **main()**, the program ends when the closing brace of **main()** is reached.

Although C functions behave like BASIC subroutines in many respects, there are differences between the two. One difference is that a RETURN statement in a C function is optional, depending on the function's purpose. The RETURN statement in Figure 1.3 is not required in C; and if it were omitted, the closing brace of the **printf()** (or any other C) function would still cause the program to return to the **main()** function. This automatic return suggests an important distinction between **main()** and other C functions:

> The closing brace of the **main()** function marks the end of the program. The closing brace of any other function marks the end of the function and returns control to whatever function called it.

One function can call another before going back to **main()**. In fact, a function can call itself. This process is a *recursive function call*. (Functions are discussed in detail in Chapter 3.)

The Standard C Library

Let's take a closer look at the **printf()** program line from Figure 1.1:

```
printf("This is my first program.\n");
```

This C program prints the message between quotation marks on the screen. The **\n** at the end of the message is called the *newline* character. It causes anything printed after the message to appear on the next (new) line. The obvious question at this point, however, is: Where is the code for the **printf()** function? We know **printf()** is used in the program, but the code doesn't appear after the closing brace or anywhere else in **main()**.

All C compilers have a *standard library*, a collection of commonly used C functions that have already been written for you, such as the **printf()** function.

If a program uses a function that is not coded as part of the program, the compiler will search through the standard library for the missing function. If the compiler finds the function in the standard library, the necessary code for that function is added to the program. (Technically, these operations are performed by the *linker*, which will be discussed later.)

The more functions you have in your compiler's standard library, the fewer functions you have to write yourself. You can add whatever new functions you like. As your standard library expands, programming in C becomes easier and easier because you don't have to rewrite functions. Eventually, even very complex programs become little more than a series of C function calls.

Note: The designers of your compiler can use whatever names they want for functions in the standard library. They are not restricted by any C syntax rules. One compiler, for example, has a function named **putfmt()** that serves the same purpose as **printf()** in most other compilers. Unfortunately, such practices reduce the portability of C programs.

Review the documentation that came with your compiler to find out what functions are included in your standard library. Don't be concerned if you don't fully understand any jargon in the discussion.

That understanding will come in due course. All you want to do now is gain some idea of the extent of your standard library. Make a note of common functions with "nonstandard" names [e.g., `putfmt()` instead of `printf()`] as you encounter them in subsequent program examples.

There is nothing "standard" about the number of functions included in the standard library. Some compilers supply a few dozen functions, whereas others have more than one hundred. Many functions in the library, however, *behave* in a "standard" way [e.g., `printf()`; see Chapter 5 for full discussion of `printf()`]. Because deviations do exist, you should review your compiler's documentation to determine how each function works.

In subsequent discussions, the term *library* refers to those functions that are part of the standard C library. It is assumed that your compiler uses the common function names, and that nonstandard function names are not a serious problem.

Semicolons in C

Now that you know where the `printf()` function comes from, we can take a more detailed look at what it does. Look at the program line:

```
printf("This is my first program.\n");
```

Notice that the line ends with a semicolon. The semicolon *marks the end of a C program statement*. In BASIC, program statements may end with a colon, a back slash, a new line number, or some other character. These characters have the same purpose in both languages: they mark where the program statement ends. Omitting the semicolon at the end of a program statement is a common mistake made by beginning C programmers.

Arguments to Functions

A function usually cannot perform a task unless it is given some information first. This information is called an *argument* of the function. Arguments are listed between the parentheses that follow the function name. In Figure 1.1, the argument of `printf()` is: "`This is my first program.\n`" which is simply a string of characters to be displayed on the screen. The **printf()** function treats any characters between quotation marks as a *string constant* for display.

Any number of arguments can be passed to a function. If more than one argument is passed, they form an *argument list* for the function. Arguments in the list must be separated by commas.

For example, a function calculating the volume of a cube needs the length, height, and width of the cube. Our hypothetical function, therefore, might appear as in Figure 1.4 below:

Figure 1.4

```
volume(l, h, w)
       .
   {
              .                  /* statements necessary to */
              .                  /* calculate the volume */

   }
```

In this figure the dots represent details of the function to be discussed later.

Figure 1.5 summarizes what we have learned about functions so far:

Figure 1.5

```
                      ┌──────────────── Argument list
                      │
                      ▼
   volume(l, h, w)    ◄──────────── Function name
   {                  ◄──────────── Start of function body
       .
       .              ◄──────────── Function body
       .
   }                  ◄──────────── End of function body
                                    and function
```

Note that a function can have no arguments passed to it; **main()** was used in this manner in Figure 1.1. You must still include parentheses, however, so that the compiler will know that you are using a function.

The use of "**This is my first program.\n**" as the argument passed to the **printf()** function in Figure 1.1 is not very different from the BASIC version in the same example. In both cases, the string constant surrounded by quotation marks gives **printf()** and PRINT the information to be displayed on the screen.

If you have written BASIC programs, you have used C-like functions before, but perhaps didn't view them as such. For example, the function **strlen(str)** in C does the same thing as LEN(S$) in BASIC: it returns the number of characters in a string variable named **str** or S$. Your library probably contains the **strlen()** function. If so, read your documentation to verify its purpose.

An Overview

Now that you know something about C functions, let's review the program in Figure 1.1, labeling all of its parts.

Figure 1.6

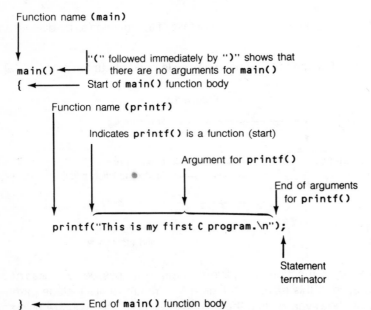

Remember that C functions can call other functions, and that a function can call itself through a recursive function call.

Programming Style

Lower- versus Upper-Case Letters

If you are accustomed to writing programs in BASIC, some parts of a C program may seem odd. For example, the syntax is different, and most C program statements are written in lower-case letters. There is a convention in C that reserves upper-case letters for *symbolic names* and *constants*, whereas everything else is written in lower-case letters. To program in C, you should develop the habit of writing in lower-case letters.

Placement of Braces and Indentation

C is a *free-form* language that doesn't care what style or format you use, as long as it is syntactically correct. The position of a statement is not important. Certain style conventions, however, make a C program easier to read. Although you are free to decide these things for yourself, some style guidelines are presented below.

Braces group program statements together and mark the beginning and end of functions. The proper indentation and placement of braces make C programs easier to read (and debug!) than they would be otherwise.

Braces *and* Functions

The opening brace for a function is placed below, and aligned with, the beginning of the *function declaration*. (For now, function declaration and function name will be used interchangeably.) The closing brace has the same alignment. For example, **main( )** is a function that is declared in the program in Figure 1.1. Note how the braces are aligned in Figure 1.7:

Figure 1.7

```
main()
{
     printf("This is my first C program. \n");
}
```

The declaration of **main( )** follows this convention because the

opening-closing braces for the **main()** function are in vertical alignment [i.e., they line up under the **m** in **main()**].

By indenting the statement that forms the body of **main()**, we can
easily see where **main()** starts and ends just by looking at the
braces. Legibility becomes more important as program complexity
increases.

Braces *in* Functions

Braces can also group statements together in functions. Suppose we
want to add **1** to the variables **x** and **y** as part of a **for** *loop*. The
following example in Figure 1.8 suggests the style that should be
used (dots represent the missing details):

Figure 1.8

```
  main()
  {
       .

       .

       for (...){          /* start of loop */
            .

            .
            x = x + 1;
            y = y + 1;
       }                    /* end of loop */
  }
```

Notice the opening brace at the end of the **for** statement. The corresponding closing brace aligns with the **f** in **for**, just as the closing
brace of the **main()** function aligns with the **m**.

Braces used in this manner tell us two things: (1) **for** is not a function, but rather a part of the C syntax (otherwise, the opening brace
would be placed on the next line under the **f** in **for**); and (2) everything between the opening and closing braces is associated with the
for loop. Braces group the statements that are controlled by the
for loop into a single *block* of code. Indentation shows what belongs
with what. (The example above is an inefficient way of incrementing
the **x** and **y** variables and is not meant to represent good C coding
practices. You will learn why later.)

The space immediately following the word **for** also indicates that it is part of the C syntax, but is not the name of a function. The compiler, however, doesn't care if the space is there or not. Although strong arguments can be made for including this space, it is usually not used in day-to-day programming. You should decide whether to use such spacing or not. Be sure to select one style and use it consistently.

Program Variables

A *variable* is a quantity that may assume any one of a set of values. Before a variable can be used in a C program, the programmer must state explicitly what type of variable it is. This is called the *declaration* of the variable. All variables *must* be declared before they can be used in a program.

C has several variable types, of which only `int` and `char` will be discussed here. (Less expensive compilers may not support all the data types C has to offer; therefore, `int` and `char` are used so that the sample programs can be run on compilers that implement only a subset of C data types as well as on others.) A *type* `int` variable is used for integer numbers, and a *type* `char` variable is used for characters. *Any variable used in a function must be declared before the first program statement.*

For example, suppose a function named `letter()` uses a variable `let_count` to count the number of letters, and `delta_let` to manipulate characters in the function. The function might appear as

Figure 1.9

```
letter()
{
     int let_count;      /* integer declaration */
     char delta_let;     /* character declaration */

     for(...){
     .
     .
     .
     }
}
```

In the function `letter()`, the variable `let_count` is declared as type `int` (i.e., an integer), and **delta_let** as type **char** (i.e., a character).

A type `int` variable typically uses 16 bits for internal storage. It is a signed value (i.e., positive or negative) that is limited to the values −32768 through +32767 (roughly 2 raised to the 15th power with one bit used as the sign bit). Because of this limitation, the programmer must give some thought to the range of possible values that type `int` variables may assume when the program is run.

Some BASICs, such as Microsoft's BASIC-80, approach variable declaration with the DEFINT and related statements. The statement DEFINT N in BASIC-80 declares that N is an integer variable and limits it to the same range of values mentioned above.

The **char** variable declaration, on the other hand, uses 8 bits for internal storage, of which only 7 are meaningful. The 128 (2 raised to the 7th power) unique values for type **char** variables describe the ASCII (American Standard for Coded Information Interchange) character set used for type **char** variables. Appendix A lists the ASCII character codes.

You can imagine the kind of trouble you can get into if you try to use a type **char** variable when you really want a type `int`. Compared to the reckless abandon of variables in most BASIC programs, variable declaration may seem a burden at first. You will quickly find, however, that variable declaration creates more efficient and maintainable code in the long run.

Variable Names

Variable names (or identifiers) consist of letters, digits, and the underscore (_), which counts as a letter. They may be any length, but only the first eight characters (at most) are treated as significant by the compiler. The first character must be a letter, and upper- and lower-case letters have different significance. For example, the variable **MAX** is not the same as the variable **max**.

There are several conventions for selecting variable names. Variable names are usually written in lower-case letters, with upper-case names reserved for symbolic constants. The underscore may be used to improve the readability of a variable name (e.g., **hat_size**).

Convention suggests using the underscore as the first letter for variable and function names in the standard library (e.g., _bit). The underscore minimizes the chances of a "collision" between function
and variable names in your library routines and those in a program.

Keywords

Certain identifiers are keywords and cannot be used as variable
names:

Table 1.1
C Keywords

auto	double	if	static
break	else	int	struct
case	entry	long	switch
char	extern	register	typedef
continue	float	return	union
default	for	sizeof	unsigned
do	goto	short	while

Each keyword will be explained as we proceed through the text. (An
exception is **entry**, which is a reserved word, but not yet implemented in C.) Although C does not permit the use of keywords as variable
names, a variable named **auto_type**, for example, is permissible
because C treats it as one word and, therefore, does not consider it
to be a keyword.

Simple Use of Variables and printf()

Now that we know how to declare numeric data in a program, let's
write a simple program to print the sum of two integer numbers.
Study the program in Figure 1.10.

Figure 1.10

```
/* add two numbers and print result */

main()
{
     int sum, x, y;

     x = 20;
     y = 30;
     sum = x + y;
     printf("The sum of %d and %d = %d", x, y, sum);
}
```

The three (type `int`) variables are declared with a single `int` declaration in this program. We could also have written:

```
int sum;
int x;
int y;
```

The multiple declaration above is common for line-oriented text editors, whereas the single declaration in Figure 1.10 is the norm for screen-oriented text editors. Pick the one you prefer.

Note that the type declaration appears first because variables must be declared before they are used. It is good programming practice to leave a blank space between the variable declaration(s) and the program statements that follow to make the type declarations easier to read.

The use of the `printf()` function in Figure 1.10 differs from that in Figure 1.1. `printf()` can do much more than just print strings. The general description of `printf()` is

```
printf("control string", argument1, argument2, ...)
```

where the *control string* can be (1) ordinary text characters, such as "**The sum of...**", or (2) *conversion characters* to specify what and how data should be printed. The lead-in character for conversion is the percent sign (%). In Figure 1.10, the `%d` specifies that the conversion be a decimal number. The arguments that follow the control string match the conversion specifications from left to right. This alignment is shown in Figure 1.11:

Figure 1.11

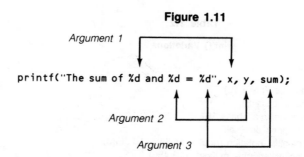

The *control string* appears between quotation marks and contains three conversion specifications indicated by the three **%d**'s in the string. These **%d**'s signal that three arguments will follow the end of the control string, each separated by a comma. Because **x** is the first argument in the list, it is printed first, followed by **y**, and finally, by the **sum**.

The variable values appear on the output device [usually a CRT (cathode ray tube, or screen)] at their respective places in the control string. For the program presented in Figure 1.10, the output would appear as

The sum of 20 and 30 = 50

Note how the value of each variable associates with its conversion character (**%d**) in the control string.

In addition to decimal conversion, the following variations can be used with **printf()**:

Table 1.2

printf() Variations

Numeric

%d   -   decimal (base 10)
%o   -   octal (base 8)
%x   -   hexadecimal (base 16)
%u   -   unsigned decimal
%e   -   scientific notation (double or float, 1.23E23)
%f   -   decimal (double or float, 123.456)
%g   -   %e or %f; select shortest

String

%c   -   single character
%s   -   string of characters

These variations will be used in later programs. [As indicated earlier, Chapter 5 presents a full discussion of **printf()**.]

Some of the BASIC counterparts for numerics are shown in the table below:

Table 1.3

BASIC Numeric Counterparts

C	BASIC-80	North Star
%4d	PRINT USING "# # # #"	!%4I
%5.2f	PRINT USING "# # # # #.# #"	!%7F2
%x	PRINT HEX$(X)	None

We told you C was better!

Style Summary

C is a free form language. That is, braces don't have to line up, spaces can be used or left out after keywords, and so on. In fact, the program in Figure 1.1 could be written as

```
main(){printf("This is my first C program.\n");}
```

and it would compile and run exactly as before. Most people, however, find a "scrunched up" program more difficult to read. Adopting some of the style suggestions in this chapter and keeping them will help you write programs that are easier to read, understand, and maintain.

Try some of the `printf()` conversions above in a program of your own. Experiment by purposely leaving out a semicolon or a brace and using an undeclared variable to see what happens. (Don't worry; it's difficult to "hurt" anything in hardware that is under software control.) Learning the kinds of error messages your compiler generates in a "controlled" situation will make program debugging easier later on.

Devote as much time as you need to becoming comfortable with the C constructs in this chapter before proceeding to the next one.

Chapter 2
Operators, Variables, and Loops

Operators are characters that designate mathematical or logical operations, such as **+**, **−**, etc. C makes an extensive set of these operators available to the programmer. Some are presented here, and others are discussed in subsequent chapters.

Operators

Arithmetic/Relational Operators

Some of the more common arithmetic and relational operators are listed below.

Table 2.1

Operator	Interpretation
Arithmetic	
+	add
−	subtract
*	multiply
/	divide
%	modulo (yields remainder of integer division)

Relational

>	greater than
>=	greater than or equal to
<	less than
<=	less than or equal to
==	equal to
!=	not equal to

These operators are straightforward except for the equality/inequality operators. BASIC uses the equal sign both for assignment (X = X + 1) and as a test for equality (IF A = B THEN ...), but C makes a distinction between the two.

The assignment operator is the same for both C and BASIC (e.g., **X = X + 1**). In a test for equality, however, C uses a double-equal sign (= =). With different operators, you can tell at a glance which operation is being performed.

The test for inequality in C is **!=** as compared to <> in most BASICs. The exclamation mark (**!**) means *not* in C.

if-else Statement

The **if-else** statement shows how a relational operator is used. The general format is:

```
if(test criterion)
        THEN do this statement if test is True;
else
        do this statement if test is False;
```

An **if-else** statement in C functions like IF-THEN-ELSE in BASIC. ("Test criterion" is used instead of the more formal "conditional expression" to reinforce the idea that a test is performed by an **if** statement to decide what the program will do next.)

The **if** statement in C does not correspond exactly to BASIC because C syntax does not use *then* as a keyword. THEN is capitalized in the general **if-else** statement to emphasize the parallel between the two languages. It is *not* part of the C language.

Let's suppose that we want to write a routine that prints **Male** if **x** is zero, but **Female** otherwise. The BASIC program might be

Figure 2.1

```
100 REM
110 REM    0= MALE    OTHERWISE FEMALE
120 REM
130 IF X=0 THEN PRINT "MALE" ELSE PRINT "FEMALE"
140 (rest of program)
```

The C version would then be

Figure 2.2

```
/* 0 = male otherwise female */
if(x==0)
    printf("Male");
else
    printf("Female");
```

The **if** statement tests the value of **x** and prints **Male** if **x** equals zero. That is, if the test condition (or conditional expression) of whether **x** equals zero is True, then the statement immediately following **if** is executed; otherwise, the **else** statement is executed.

Two or more statements can be grouped together with braces. The compiler treats multiple statements after **if-else** as a single statement when they are enclosed by braces, and executes them as a single unit.   For example, if we want to increment a variable to count the number of males and females, we can alter the routine in Figure 2.2, as shown in Figure 2.2a.

Figure 2.2a

```
/* 0 = male otherwise female and count each */
    if(x==0){
        printf("Male");
        is_male=is_male + 1;
    } else {
        printf("Female");
        is_female=is_female + 1;
    }
```

If **x** does not equal zero, *neither* the **printf("Male")** *nor* the incrementing of **is_male** will be executed. If the braces are removed, is_male will always be incremented. In fact, the program would not compile because the else would no longer be tied to its if. Why? If braces are not used with an if-else statement, *only the first statement after the* if *and* else *is affected by the test criterion.*

Also note the spaces before and after else.

```
} else {
```

Placement of Braces with if-else

The program in Figure 2.2a illustrates several style conventions used in C. Notice how the braces are used when if-else has compound statements. Convention suggests that the opening brace for the if statement be on the same line as if, and that the closing brace be aligned with the i in if.

The else statement follows the same format. The opening brace is on the same line as else, and the closing brace is aligned with the closing brace of the if. If there were no compound statement with if, the closing brace would align with the e in else, as in Figure 2.2b:

Figure 2.2b

```
if(x= =0)
    printf("male");
else {
    printf("female");
    is_female=is_female + 1;
}
```

Figure 2.2c summarizes the **if-else** style conventions for compound statements:

Figure 2.2c

```
if(test criteria) {
        True: then do these compound statements;
} else {
        False: do these compound statements;
}
```

Try the routine in Figure 2.2a with and without the braces to see what happens. (*Suggestion*: Add a line to the program that prints out the values of `is_male` and `is_female`.) How does the compiler handle the `else`?

Logical Operators

C has a complete range of logical operators, which is summarized below.

Table 2.2

Logical Operators

Operator	Interpretation
&&	AND
||	OR
<<	shift left
>>	shift right
!	logical negation
~	one's complement
&	bitwise AND
|	bitwise OR
^	bitwise exclusive OR
-	unary minus

Note: Our discussion centers on AND, OR, and logical negation. (The other logical operators are discussed later.) Not all logical operators are available on the less expensive compilers.

For logical operations in C, if a test criterion or conditional expression evaluates to 0, then the test is considered logic False. Any nonzero value is logic True. To illustrate this, we could rewrite the routine in Figure 2.2 as

Figure 2.3

```
/* male if 0, female otherwise */

if(x)
     printf("Female");
else
     printf("Male");
```

The test criterion has been changed from $x == 0$ to just x. The interpretation, therefore, is that if x is True (nonzero), the value for x must be nonzero and **female**. This modification reverses the way **Male** and **Female** are handled in the program: **Female** is now printed if the test criterion is True.

In its complete form, the program might be

Figure 2.4

```
main()
{
     int x;
     x = 0;
     if(x)
           printf("Female");
     else
           printf("Male");
}
```

Because **x** has been assigned a value of zero, **Male** is printed. Why? The value of zero is a logic False value for **x**. When the test evaluates to logic False, the first statement following the **if** is skipped, and the **else** is executed.

Although this format may seem to be a complicated way of doing things, you will see it often in C programs. Try the program in Figure 2.4 to verify that it works as described.

Variables: Incrementing/Decrementing in C

Adding or subtracting the value one from a variable is so common that C has a set of special operators for just this task. Figure 2.5 shows the program from Figure 2.2a after being rewritten with these special operators.

Figure 2.5

```
/* program to print male-female and increment count */
main()
{
     int x, is_female, is_male;

     is_female = 0;
     is_male = 0;
     x = 0;
     if(x){
          printf("Female");
          ++is_female;
     } else {
          printf("Male");
          ++is_male;
     }
}
```

The notation **++is_female** is the equivalent of **is_female = is_female + 1; is_female** is incremented by one. To subtract one from **is_female**, you would use **--is_female**. To summarize:

++n;	Increments variable **n** by 1
--n;	Decrements variable **n** by 1

It is important to note that incrementing/decrementing occurs *before* any other logical operation. This means that variable **n** is incremented or decremented before it is "used" in the program. For example, if **is_female** is 99 when the routine is entered, the program statement:

```
x = ++is_female;
```

would assign **x** the value of 100 because **is_female** is incremented *before* its value is assigned to **x**. When **++** appears before the variable name, it is a *pre-increment* operator.

What happens if you want to increment **is_female** *after* **x** is assigned? The program statement:

```
x = is_female++;
```

assigns the current value of **is_female** to **x** and *then* increments **is_female**. If **is_female** were 99 coming into this statement, **x** now equals 99, and **is_female** is 100. When **+ +** appears *after* the variable name, it is a *post-increment* operator. The *post-decrement* operator works the same way and would be written:

```
x = is_female--;
```

which would decrement **is_female** after **x** has been assigned.

To test your understanding of how the pre- and post-increment/decrement operators work, would it make any difference which one we used in Figure 2.5? [Try assigning any nonzero value to **x** and then adding a **printf()** to print the value of **x**, using the pre- and post-decrement operators.]

The compiler performs increment and decrement operations according to the type of data being used. Most implementations of C use 16 bits (two bytes on a microcomputer) of storage for each integer number. Let's suppose that the integer numbers are in an array named **x**. If we want to increment the contents of the **x[1]** array element, we can use **+ +x[1]** operation. The compiler will keep track of which byte is incremented.

C also allows you to increment/decrement memory addresses. (See Chapter 4 for more information.) If a variable **x** contains the address of **p[1]**, and you want the address of **p[2]**, a **+ +x** will appear to increment **x** by one. The variable **x** must actually be incremented by two, however, because integer numbers require two bytes for storage. To get the next number in the array, you must increment the *address* by two. Fortunately, the compiler takes care of this adjustment for you. For the moment, remember that increment/decrement operations for variables with memory addresses are "scaled" according to the type of data being used.

Loops

Looping is the repetition of a group of program instructions until a particular condition is reached. C provides for several loop constructs.

while Loops

A **while** loop executes a group of program statements as long as a test criterion is True. The basic format for this loop is

```
while(test criteria True){
     execute these statements;
}
```

Braces are needed only if compound statements are controlled by the **while** statement. These braces serve the same purpose as the ones in **if-else** and **for** statements.

The following program uses the **while** construct to increment a variable from 0 to 30,000.

Figure 2.6

```
/* increment variable to 30000 */
#define  BELL 7  /* ASCII code for terminal bell */
main()
{
     int x;

     putchar(BELL);

     x = 0;
     while(x != 30000)
          ++x;

     putchar(BELL);
     printf("Loop finished\nat the bell.");
}
```

The new statements in Figure 2.6 will be explained as they appear in the program.

#define

The **#define** statement defines a *symbolic constant* for use in the program. In this case, the ASCII code that rings your computer terminal's bell (or buzzer) is defined as **BELL**. (See Appendix A for the ASCII codes.) The **#define** statement makes the compiler substitute an ASCII 7 into the program wherever it finds the symbolic constant **BELL**.

The #define statement can also be used to produce a single-byte bit pattern in octal. The general format is

```
'\nnn'
```

where nnn is the octal (base 8) number that corresponds to the desired bit pattern. (The Appendix to this chapter explains both the octal and hexadecimal numbering systems.) For the ASCII bell code in octal, we could have written:

```
#define BELL '\007'
```

The advantage of using #define is that you can change the constant's definition by changing the #define BELL, rather than searching through the entire program to alter each occurrence. Therefore, it is good practice to place #defines at the beginning of your program.

putchar(c)

The putchar(c) function is a part of the C library that is used to write a single character (the argument c in the function) to the standard output device (usually the CRT). C does not provide for input or output statements as part of the language; they are library functions.

The printf() statement can also be used to ring the terminal bell:

```
printf("%c",BELL);
```

(Remember that the %c option to printf() is used to print a single character on the output device. In this case, it would sound the bell on the terminal.)

Because the while statement controls one program statement (e.g., ++x), braces are not needed. As the program executes, the test criterion (x != 30000) is checked after each pass through the loop. When the test proves False, and x equals 30,000, control passes to the putchar() and printf() functions, and the program ends.

If the test criterion is False on entry into the loop, the statements controlled by the while will not be executed. It is possible, therefore, that statement(s) controlled by a while loop will not be executed at all.

Special printf() Characters

If you look closely at the `printf()` statement in Figure 2.6, you will see \na t in the quoted string. When you run the program, the printed message is

```
Loop finished
at the bell.
```

The \n is an escape sequence for a character constant called a *newline* character that sends a carriage-return, line-feed sequence to the output device. (The newline escape sequence serves the same purpose as a single PRINT statement in BASIC.)

Other common sequences are \t for a tab and \b for backspace. Try substituting these two sequences for the \n in the program to see their effect on the output. What happens, and why?

Escape sequences are *single* characters. The backslash is a "lead-in" for the compiler. It tells the compiler that what follows is a special character. [In this sense, the backslash functions like the conversion character (%) in `printf()`.]

When the compiler encounters the backslash, it reads the next character and substitutes the appropriate ASCII value for the character. For example, the \b (backspace) sequence is changed to a decimal 8 in ASCII, and the \t (tab) becomes a decimal 9. Both are single characters when the compiler is finished. After the backslash has served its "information" purpose, it is discarded by the compiler.

do-while Loops

The `do-while` loop is constructed like a simple `while` statement:

Figure 2.7

```
do{
    statement(s);
} while(test criterion);
```

Because the test criterion is evaluated at the bottom of the `do-while` loop, the *statement in the loop is always executed at least once*. If the test criterion is True, then the statement is executed again.

The closing brace for the **do-while** loop is placed immediately before the **while** statement. This is good practice even when only one statement is controlled by the **while** loop, because leaving out braces makes it easy to forget about the **do** lurking above.

Rewrite the program in Figure 2.6 using a **do-while** statement. Does this revision have any effect on the program?

for Loops

The **for** loop in C differs from its BASIC counterpart in that all the relevant information is in one place. As a first step towards understanding this difference, let's write the BASIC equivalent of Figure 2.6.

Figure 2.8

```
100 X = 0:REM                          (1)          (2)
110 FOR J = 0 TO 30000:REM    STEP INITIAL & TERMINAL VALUES
120 X = X + 1
130 NEXT J:REM                TEST FOR ANOTHER PASS
140 END:REM                   (3)
```

There are three functional parts in a FOR-TO-NEXT loop. The *first* part initializes the loop control variable J, which is set to 0 in line 110. The *second* part indicates the terminal value of J for the loop—30000 in this case. The *third*, and less obvious, part tests the loop control variable J to determine whether it has reached the terminal value.

The NEXT J statement in BASIC increments J. (With the STEP function, you can increment the loop control variable by some value other than one.) NEXT J then compares the loop control variable with the terminal value to determine if the loop should be executed again. If so, control is sent to line 120 until the terminal value is reached.

The **for** loop in C places all three parts in the **for** statement itself and, as a bonus, makes them visible to the programmer in one place. The terms explained in the paragraph above can be presented as follows:

Figure 2.9

```
        (1)              (2)              (3)
for( initialized value(s); test criteria; loop increment ){
            statements controlled by loop;
    }
```

The *first* part (1) of the **for** loop uses an assignment expression for one or more variables. If more than one variable is initialized, each must be separated by a comma. The *second* part (2) uses some form of relational or logical operation (e.g., **!=**, **==**, **<=**, etc.). The test criterion may be complex (e.g., involving a logical AND, OR, etc.). The *third* (3) part of the loop often consists of incrementing one or more variables, but other expressions can be used.

The C equivalent of the loop in Figure 2.8 is:

Figure 2.10

```
int x, j;

x = 0;
for(j = 0; j <= 30000; ++j)
     ++x;
```

Referring to the assignment and relational operators, you can see that **j** is initialized to **0**. (Assignment uses a single equal sign.) This expression is the equivalent of part (1) in the FOR-TO-NEXT loop. It establishes the initial value(s) for the loop.

The test criterion compares **j** to the terminal value (2) **30000** (**!=** tests for inequality). This comparison corresponds to the test performed by the NEXT of a FOR-TO-NEXT loop in BASIC.

The third (3) part of the loop increments the controlling variable (i.e., **++j**). As long as **j** does not equal **30000** (i.e., the test is True), the statements controlled by the loop are executed. All three parts of the C loop structure are visible to the programmer *in one place*.

Remember that the test criterion *must* be a relational or logical operation. If the test is for equality, it must use the double-equal sign. From the example above, a common mistake is

```
for(j = 0; j = 30000; ++j)
```

In this case, **30000** is assigned to **j** each time the **for** loop is executed. As a result, the test condition of the **for** loop (**j = 30000**) will always be true, the maximum value **j** will reach is 30001, and the **for** loop will execute forever.

Not all compilers catch this error. The test criterion should be written with the relational operator: **j == 30000**. This kind of error becomes less likely as you gain experience with C.

The **for** loop in C is more flexible than its BASIC counterpart. For example, you could move the incrementing of **x** into the **for** statement itself. The new lines would be

```
for(j = 0; j != 30000; ++j, ++x)
      ;                 /* A do-nothing statement */
```

The statement terminator (the semicolon) is necessary because a **for** loop must control at least one program statement. In this case, it is a *null*, or "do-nothing," statement.

When a **for** loop controls a compound statement, braces must be used; but when it controls a single statement, no braces are needed.

Notice that the three major parts of the loop are separated by *semicolons*, and that any additional arguments to a part of the loop are separated by *commas*. (The **++j** and **++x** must be separated by a comma.) Would the following code accomplish the same task?

Figure 2.11

```
int x;

for(x = 0; x != 30000; x++)
      ;
```

Try it and see.

C also differs from BASIC in that more than one variable can be initialized at a time. If we wanted to preserve the distinction between the loop counter **j** and a variable **x**, we could rewrite the loop as

Figure 2.12

```
int j, x;
for(j = 0, x = 0; j != 30000; j++, x++)
    ;
```

In this instance, both **j** and **x** are initialized by the assignment expressions in the first part of the loop. Each initialized variable must be separated by a comma.

It is also possible to omit the expressions for all three parts of the loop in C. In this case, the test criterion always evaluates as True, resulting in an infinite loop. That is, the statement **for(;;)** would execute forever, unless one of the statements controlled by the loop caused control to branch out of the loop.

One common bug you may encounter with the **for** loop is the following (assuming **y** is assigned before the loop):

Figure 2.13

```
int sum, x, y;
sum = 0;
y = 5;
for(x = 1; x <= y; x++);    /* <-- big trouble */
        sum = sum + x * y;
```

The semicolon after the **for** loop essentially says that we have a do-nothing loop, when we really want to calculate the sum of the **x** and **y** products. With C's free-form syntax, it makes no difference where you put the semicolon when you enter the program. The formatting style—not the compiler—helps you read the code.

What the code above actually does is clearer when it is written as

Figure 2.14

```
int sum, x, y;
sum = 0;
y = 5;
for(x = 1; x <= y; x++)
    ;
sum = sum + x * y;
```

which is not what we actually want. sum equals 25 in this case. (Why?) This makes the bug just that much worse: the program runs and generates a nonzero value for sum. Never place a null statement on the same line as the for loop.

break, Exiting a Loop

Loops examine a set of data until a specified value causes the loop to be exited. The break statement allows us to exit a for, while, or do-while loop before the terminal value is reached.

Figure 2.15 is a simple example of how the break statement is used.

Figure 2.15

```
main()
{
    int x;

    x = 0;

    for(; ; ++x){
        if(x >= 30000)
            break;
    }

    printf("%d",x);
}
```

In this example, the for loop is set up as an infinite loop, but it also increments x with each pass through the loop. The if statement tests if x is greater than or equal to 30000 (the test criterion requires a relational, not assignment, operator) on each pass through the loop. If the test is False, the loop continues to increment x because the break statement is not executed.

Eventually, x equals 30000, which causes the break to execute and sends control to the next statement "outside" the loop. (Note the use of braces with the for loop. Try running the program without them. What happens? Why?) If all goes well, the printf() displays the value of x on the CRT.

continue, Ignoring Code within a Loop

Let's suppose that you have a home alarm system that is monitored by a C program, and that a function called **monitor()** scans a number of alarm devices and reports to the program. In all cases except the number **999**, everything is taken to be okay with the alarm system. When the number **999** is received, however, the program initiates a complex procedure that does everything from turning on the lights to calling the police.

In this situation, we don't want a statement that breaks us out of the loop. We simply want to bypass the alarm section of the code, unless we receive a **999**.

The routine in Figure 2.16 illustrates how the **continue** statement might be used.

Figure 2.16

```
for(; ;){
    if(monitor() != 999)
        continue;

    /* turn on lights, sound alarm, call police */

}
```

An infinite loop continually monitors the alarm system by repeated calls to **monitor()**. Many modern office buildings use such a loop for automated heating and cooling.

The call to **monitor()** returns a number, of which only **999** indicates a problem. As long as **monitor()** does not return a **999**, the **if** statement is True, and the **continue** statement is executed. The **continue** statement causes the next pass through the infinite loop, calls to **monitor()**, and bypasses the complex code that activates the alarm system.

You can avoid the **continue** statement by rewriting the program as follows:

Figure 2.17

```
for(; ;){
    if(monitor() == 999)
        break;
}
/* turn on lights, sound alarm, call police */
```

In Figure 2.17, we stay in the infinite loop as long as **monitor()** doesn't return a **999**. When it does, we exit the **for** loop and activate the alarm system. The **break** statement makes your code more direct and easier to understand. For some alarm systems, however, the **continue** statement is a better choice.

Because loops are used frequently in programming, try all the examples in this chapter before moving on. Experiment with different loop constructs (e.g., leaving braces out, adding **printf()** statements, and so on) to get a "feel" for them. After you have tried variations of the routines provided, create some of your own. Check your compiler's library to see if there are any functions that may be useful in your own program creations.

Appendix 2
Octal and Hexadecimal
Numbering Systems

Despite all the things a computer can do, it only understands two things: on and off (or 1 and 0). In other words, a computer understands only data presented in base 2, or binary. Although this format is convenient for the computer, it doesn't work too well for people who are used to working with decimal (base 10) arithmetic.

Base 8 (octal) and base 16 (hexadecimal) numbering systems are often used for communicating with a computer. We saw in the last chapter that character constants can be represented in octal form. Before we discuss the octal and hexadecimal numbering systems, however, we must first consider binary numbers.

Binary Numbering System

Only two states are possible when working in binary: on and off. The *on* state, represented as a 1, is usually some positive reference voltage in the computer (e.g., plus 5 volts). The *off* state is represented as a 0 (e.g., 0 volts). The following discussion uses the ASCII character set as a point of reference because it is used frequently in C.

The ASCII (American Standard for Coded Information Interchange) character set uses 7 data bits. Defining bit 0 as the least significant bit, ASCII characters use only bits 0 through 6, a total of 7 bits. For example, a typical microcomputer uses an 8-bit data bus to communicate data throughout the system. However, when the microcomputer uses the ASCII character set, the high bit (i.e., bit 7) is usually ignored, or stripped away. Therefore, when we talk about ASCII characters, we are actually concerned with bits 0 though 6; the high bit is not used.

Each bit can be either on or off at any given moment. There are, therefore, 256 (i.e., 2^8) possible distinct patterns in an 8-bit data word. Each bit can be thought of as 2 raised to a power, as shown in Figure 2A.1.

Figure 2A.1

power	2^7	2^6	2^5	2^4	2^3	2^2	2^1	2^0
Binary:	0	1	0	0	0	0	0	1
Decimal:	128	64	32	16	8	4	2	1
position	7	6	5	4	3	2	1	0

In Figure 2A.1, each bit has a numeric value that equals 2 raised to a power equal to its bit position. The decimal values are listed to make the relationship clearer.

When the high bit is not used, the largest number we can represent in the ASCII character set is 127. Because 0 is also included in the set, 128 different bit patterns are available for the ASCII character set.

In Figure 2A.1, the bits in positions 0 and 6 (numbering starts with 0 and reads from right to left) are on, which means that the decimal numbers 64 and 1 are "turned on," for a total of 65. If you look up this figure in the ASCII table in Appendix A, you will find that decimal 65 is the ASCII code for the letter A. The binary representation for A is 01000001. (Notice that the high bit is off.)

Unfortunately, people don't think in terms of binary numbers, which makes communication with the computer that much more difficult. In an attempt to make things easier on us, other numbering systems are often used: octal (base 8) and hexadecimal (base 16).

Octal Numbering System

The octal numbering system divides binary digits into fields of 3 bits each, starting with the low (i.e., 0) data bit. If you refer to Figure 2A.2, you will see that 3 bits let us represent 8 numbers (0 through 7).

Figure 2A.2

Binary	Octal
000	0
001	1
010	2
011	3
100	4
101	5
110	6
111	7

Obviously, we need to be able to count higher than 7. If we want a number larger than 7, we must "roll over" into the next field of 3 digits. The binary digits 8, 9, and 63 are shown below.

Figure 2A.3

Field 2	Field 1	= 6 bits total
001	000	= 8
001	001	= 9
111	111	= 63

To represent a number greater than 63, we must go to a third field. However, because 8 bits is the width of our data world, the third field can use only 2 bits. Therefore, the largest octal number possible in the third field is 3. The binary, octal, and decimal representations for the 3 fields are shown in Figure 2A.4.

Figure 2A.4

	Field 3	Field 2	Field 1	
Binary	11	111	111	11111111
Octal	3	7	7	377
Decimal	128+64	+32+16+8	+4+2+1 =	255
Binary	01	000	001	01000001
Octal	1	0	1	101
Decimal	64 +	0 +	1 =	65

As you can see, binary 01000001 is 101 in octal, and 65 in decimal. Again, this is the ASCII representation for the letter A.

To use the character constant A in C, you might write:

```
#define LETTER_A  '\101'
```

Appendix A lists the ASCII codes in the binary, octal, and decimal numbering systems. The most significant advantage of octal over binary is that the same information can be conveyed in 3 digits rather than 8.

Hexadecimal Numbering System

Hexadecimal ("hex" from now on) is a base 16 numbering system that uses 2 fields of 4 binary digits for each hex number. Because we must be able to count from 0 through 15, we encounter a problem when we try to represent the numbers 10 through 15 as single characters. For this reason, the letters A through F are used to represent the numbers 10 through 15, as shown in Figure 2A.5.

Figure 2A.5

Binary	Hex	Decimal
0000	0	0
0001	1	1
0010	2	2
0011	3	3
0100	4	4
0101	5	5
0110	6	6
0111	7	7
1000	8	8
1001	9	9
1010	A	10
1011	B	11
1100	C	12
1101	D	13
1110	E	14
1111	F	15

To represent a number larger than 15, we must again "roll over" into the next hex field. The binary-hex representation for 16 is

Figure 2A.6

```
0001   0000

  1      0   = 16 (decimal)
```

Therefore, *a 10 hex is 16 decimal.* Note the base 2 power relationship, as presented in Figure 2A.1. That is, 2 raised to the fourth power is 16.

Problems can arise, however. If you see "10" written somewhere, how can you tell if the number represents 10 decimal or 10 hex? Octal is less of a problem, especially when all 3 fields are represented (e.g., 012 is 10 decimal). Because of this potential area of confusion, C expects to find **0x** before a hex number. To use a hex constant of 16, we would write it in the program as **0x10**.

If we want to define the same constant in octal, we must supply a leading 0. *In octal, a decimal 10 is defined as 012.* Therefore, an ASCII Escape character is *27 decimal, 0x1b hex, or 033 octal.* For the letter A, we find:

Figure 2A.7

01000001	(binary)	=	A	(ASCII)
1 0 1	(octal)	=	A	
4 1	(hex)	=	A	
64 + 1 = 65² (decimal)		=	A	

The hex number 0x41 is the ASCII representation of the letter A. You should be able to verify that the largest 8-bit number in hex is FF, which corresponds to 255 decimal. This also means that

     377 (octal) = FF (hex) = 255 (decimal)

One advantage of hexadecimal numbers is that 2 hex numbers can represent 8 binary digits; hex numbers are shorter. Because hex numbers use fields of 4 binary digits, numeric representations in hex are easier since computers use address and data fields that are even multiples of 4 bits. (Microcomputers typically use 16 bits for the address and 8 bits for data.)

You may want to review Appendix A to reinforce the concepts discussed here.

Chapter 3
Writing Your Own Functions

One of C's strong points is that new functions can be created and used over and over again in different programs. Once a function has been written and tested, it need not be written again. It becomes part of your "personal" C library. Some of the ground rules for writing and using functions are discussed below.

Form of C Functions

If you have a compiler that supports data types other than `int` and `char`, you probably noticed when you reviewed the functions in your standard library that they appear more "complex" than those discussed so far. It is not that the functions are more complex, but that we have not gone beyond a simple call to the function. Until now, functions have been hidden in the dark of a black box called the standard library. It's time to bring them to light.

Obviously, you must create a function before you can use it. In more formal terms, you need to define the function. *All C function definitions have the following general form:*

Figure 3.1

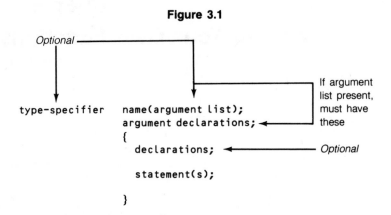

Although this form may seem intimidating at first, it really is not. To make the definition more concrete, let's assume that we need a simple function to cube a number passed to the function. Let's use a crude function first, then make it more intelligent later.

Figure 3.2

```
/* this is a function that cubes an integer number */

int cube(number)
int number;
{
      number = number * number * number;
      return(number);
}
```

The first line of the function gives us the following information:

Figure 3.3

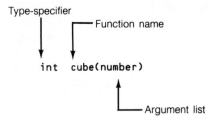

Type-Specifier

A *type-specifier* indicates what type of data is returned from the function. A type-specifier must be used when the function returns a data type other than an integer. C provides for many data types (e.g., `char`, `double`, `float`, `long` and `short int`, plus others). For the time being, we shall stick with the simple data types, `int` and `char`.

If you omit the type-specifier from your function definition, it is assumed that you want an integer. When you write a function to return a character from the function, the compiler converts the character to an integer anyway. Therefore, the *default type-specifier* for a function is `int`. Any function definition that does not include a type-specifier defaults to a function that returns an `int`.

Given what you have just learned, you really do not need the type-specifier for the function in Figure 3.2. If we omitted the type-specifier, the function would default to an integer function anyway. If the function were designed to return a floating-point number (i.e., a number that might have a fractional value), a `float` type-specifier would be needed.

This default points out one potential trouble spot. If a function is to return something other than an integer, but the type-specifier is left out of the function definition, you will probably get "garbage" back from the function. Even worse, the function may return reasonable values in one case, but garbage in another. Remember that the absence of a type-specifier may be the cause if a function seems to have a mind of its own!

Function Names

In our cube example, we gave the function the clever *function name* of `cube`. Generally, the character representation of a function name follows the same rules for variable names: (1) it must start with a letter or underscore character, (2) digits are permitted after the first letter, and (3) only the first eight characters are significant. The third rule may be a potential problem area. Often three steps are required to produce an executable C program. The sequence can be viewed as follows:

```
source  -> compiler -> assembler -> linker -> executable
program     (8)          (5)          (7)      program
```

This diagram indicates that the compiler recognizes eight significant characters for variable and function names in the source program, but that the assembler is limited to five characters, and the linker to seven.

Now suppose that you have the following function declarations in your program:

Figure 3.4

```
on_val1(a)                      on_val2(b)
int a;                          int b;
{                               {
        .                               .
        .                               .
}                               }
```

Perhaps the functions are used to turn on valves 1 and 2 in some control process. The compiler can distinguish between the two function declarations because it has eight significant characters for function names. Even the linker can tell the difference despite its limitation of seven characters.

The assembler is the problem because both functions appear to have the function name **on_va**. The assembler will issue a duplicate definition (or its equivalent) error message. You should check your compiler's documentation to determine what the actual limit is for function and variable names; it may be more or less restrictive than the example presented here.

There is one additional requirement, however: the function name must have opening and closing parentheses. These enable the compiler to distinguish between a variable and a function name. To the compiler, **main** is a variable, whereas **main()** is a function.

When you write a function, the semicolon (**;**) should not appear after the function name. By omitting the semicolon, you tell the compiler that you are *defining* the function, not using it.
The line

```
    int cube(number)        /*correct way*/
```

informs the compiler that you are defining the function cube.

The line

```
    int cube(number);            /*wrong way*/
```

will produce a syntax error on some compilers, and even stranger errors on others.

Argument List

An *argument list* contains the variables that pass to the function any information needed to perform its task. The argument list may contain zero or more arguments. In the examples presented so far, we have seen `main()` use no arguments, `volume(l,h,w)` use three arguments, and `cube(number)` use one argument. Whether a function needs an argument depends on the purpose of the function. A function that requires "outside" help needs an argument list. If the function is self-contained and needs no information other than what it creates itself, no argument list is necessary. (You will learn later in this chapter why this is true.)

Argument Declarations

Each variable in the argument list of a function must have an *argument declaration*. If there is no argument list for a function, there is no argument declaration. To illustrate this, let's compare the `main()` and `cube()` function examples.

Figure 3.5

main() function	vs.	cube() function

```
    main()                      int cube(number)
    {                           int number;
            .                   {
            .                           .
    }                                   .
                                }
```

Although thus far, `main()` has not needed any arguments, `cube()` needs to know the number that is to be cubed. Because a number is "handed" to the `cube()` function from "outside" itself, `cube()` needs to know what type of data it has just received. This communication is the purpose of the argument declarations.

Any variable in an argument list that is not explicitly declared defaults automatically to an `int`; this is known as a *default argument declaration*. To avoid future problems, you should develop the habit of explicitly declaring *all* arguments in a function call, even when they are integer variables. There will be less chance of your forgetting to declare nonintegers if you declare all variables. Therefore, you should ignore the default and declare explicitly all function arguments. In the program examples, all arguments are declared explicitly, even when they are integers.

A semicolon follows each line of an argument list declaration. For example,

Figure 3.6

```
/*right*/                               /*wrong*/

int cube(number)                        int cube(number)
int number;   /* note semicolon */      int number     /* semi-
                                                  colon missing */

{                                       {

}                                       }
int volume(l,h,w)                       int volume(l,h,w)
int l,h,w;                              int l,h,w,
{                                       {

}                                       }
```

For the **cube()** function, a semicolon follows the single argument declaration. For **volume**, we have declared **l**, **h**, and **w** to be integers and grouped them into one argument declaration. The last argument in the group, **w**, is followed by a semicolon. Omitting the semicolon or substituting a comma is unacceptable and will produce an error when the program is compiled.

Finally, the argument declarations must occur *before the opening brace of the function body*. If we stretch things a bit, we can view everything between the opening and closing braces (i.e., the function body) as being "created" by the function, and everything else as being "handed" to the function. It seems only logical, therefore, to have the arguments that have been handed to the function declared before the function body.

Function Body

The opening brace marks the beginning of the function body, and the closing brace marks the end of (1) the function body and (2) the function definition. The declarations and statements needed to perform the function's task are located in the function body.

All variables in the function body that were not declared as part of the argument list declarations must be declared in the function body itself before they are used. If, for example, a function uses variable j as a loop counter in the function body, an `int j;` declaration must appear in the function body before j is used, as in the following:

Figure 3.7

```
junk(stuff)      /* Function name and argument list  */
int stuff;       /* Argument declaration             */
{                /* Start of function body           */

    int j;       /* Internal variable declaration    */
    .
    ..
}                /* End function body and definition  */
```

The variable **stuff** is handed to the function as part of the argument list and must be declared before the start of the function body (i.e., the opening brace). The variable j is used internally by the function; j does not need any "outside" help to do its task in the function body. Therefore, j is declared in the function body (i.e., between the opening and closing braces).

In our **cube()** example, **number** is the only variable used in the function body. Because **number** was declared as an argument declaration, it need not be declared again. Indeed, a second declaration of **number** will draw an error message from the compiler.

The return Statement in C

The RETURN statement in BASIC sends program control back to the point in the program that called the subroutine. A simple **return** statement in C does the same thing. If a C function does not have a **return** statement in it, a simple **return** is performed when the closing brace of the function is encountered.

For example, if we want a simple function that will pause for the user to press a key before continuing, we can use either of the two versions presented in Figure 3.8.

Figure 3.8

```
pause_1()                              pause_2()
{                                      {
    int c;                                 int c;

    c = getchar();                         c = getchar();
    return;                            }

}
```

Neither function needs outside data passed to it to perform its task, so there is no argument list or declaration. We do, however, use variable **c** in the function body, so **c** must be declared before it is used.

The function **getchar()** is a common library function used to get a single character from the keyboard. (There are several reasons why **c** is an **int**, which will be explained in Chapter 8. For now, we shall abide by the compiler's documentation, which says that **c** must be an **int**.)

Although the function **pause_1()** makes explicit use of the **return** statement, **pause_2()** does not. However, because the closing brace of the function body is found after the call to **getchar()**, **pause_2()** also returns to the calling program—both programs perform identically.

Returning a Value from a Function

The **return** in C is not limited to a simple return from the function; it can also pass a value back to the code that called the function. If we replace the **return** in **pause_1()** with the following statement:

```
return(c);
```

we can return whatever key was struck by the user to the code that called **pause_1()**. Any expression can be contained between the parentheses [i.e., **return(x + y)**]. The expression can be as complex as you want, but only one value will be returned.

To test yourself, what data type is returned from **pause_1( )**? (*Hint*: what does the type-specifier for the function say? And if it doesn't say anything, what does that tell you?)

Now that you have some idea of what a function is, you may be wondering why an argument list is needed in the first place. After all, in our **cube( )** example, **number** already exists in **main( )**, so why all of the mumbo jumbo about passing arguments? This is the subject of the next section.

Scope, Storage Class, and the Longevity of Variables

Variables in C differ in behavior from those in most BASICs. In a BASIC program, a variable retains its value throughout the program. That is, it is a "global" variable.

For example, if you set X to equal 3 at the beginning of a BASIC program, then call a subroutine that assigns X the value of 5, X will be "globally" changed to have a value of 5 throughout the BASIC program. Even if X is never used after its first assignment, it will still retain the assigned value for the entire program, and its value will be present everywhere in the program.

This "globality" of BASIC variables is also a fruitful area for program bugs. How many times have you changed the value of some variable only to find that it produced some other, undesired, "side effect" (i.e., "bug") elsewhere in the program? If you've ever written a BASIC program where you felt you were running out of variable names, you've probably experienced such bugs. These side effects can be minimized in C.

C has four *variable storage classes*: (1) *external* (**extern**), (2) *automatic* (**auto**), (3) **static**, and (4) **register**. The scope of variables will also be considered as we proceed. The *scope* of a variable refers to the part(s) of a program for which the variable is visible or available for use. To appreciate what scope actually means, however, we need to consider some of the things a compiler does when it generates a C program.

Compiler and Linker

We cannot do justice here to the inner workings of a compiler. It will serve our purposes, however, to highlight a few things that a compiler does.

The first step in writing a C program or function module is to use a text editor to type the C program. After you finish writing a program, you can save it on disk as **source.c**, which becomes the source code for the program. The *source code* is really little more than a text file with statements that are (we hope) in agreement with the rules of C.

The text file **source.c** becomes the input file to the C compiler. The compiler checks the source file to make sure that the file agrees with the syntactic and semantic rules of C. If it does not, then the compiler will generate error messages to help you locate and correct the errors. For example, suppose you write a program like the one in Figure 3.9:

Figure 3.9

```
main()              /* not a good program */
{
     int sum, price;

     sum = price * quantity;
     printf("\nThe sum is %d", sum);

}
```

The compiler will generate an error message because the variable **quantity** has not been defined. You and I know that we want **quantity** to be an integer, but the compiler doesn't know that. The compiler must generate an error message because it doesn't know how to reference **quantity**. It doesn't know what type of variable **quantity** is, what it should contain, or anything else about it.

If **quantity** were defined in the proper manner in the program in Figure 3.9, where would the **printf()** function come from? We already know that **printf()** comes from the library of C functions, but how does **printf()** get "tied in" with the program? To simplify this process, the compiler tells itself: "I've found **printf()** and it's a function. I'll store some preliminary stuff about it now and let someone else worry about the details.''

After the compiler finishes examining the source file and finds that everything is okay, it outputs an intermediate file. (Let's call it `source.int`.) The contents of the intermediate file will vary among compilers, but might be some form of intermediate language (e.g., pseudocode) developed by the designer of the compiler, or assembly language. It's not necessary to know the specific contents.

The intermediate file (e.g., `source.int`) becomes the input file for the linker. The primary purpose of the *linker* is to take all of the information generated by the compiler and ''link'' that information together to form an executable C program. The linker is the ''someone else'' for whom the compiler generated the preliminary information about `printf()`.

What happens when the linker comes to `printf()`? Depending on the compiler, it will have generated the information needed by the linker to resolve the missing `printf()` function. Typically, the compiler will direct the linker to look in the C library for the code necessary to complete the `printf()` function.

The important thing to remember is that the compiler must communicate to the linker the way in which missing variables or functions needed in the program are to be handled. Keep this fact in mind when you read about the scope and storage classes of variables and functions in the next section.

External Variables

External describes a storage class that can be applied to either variables or functions. *Any variable that is defined outside of a function is an external variable.* Because you cannot define a function in another function, *all C functions have an external storage class.* Consider the (skeletal) program in Figure 3.10.

Figure 3.10

```
int x;

main()
{
    x = 1;
    printf("x = %d\n", x);
    func1();
    printf("x = %d\n", x);
    func2();
    printf("x = %d\n", x);
    func3();
    printf("x = %d\n", x);
}
func1()          /* multiply x by 1 */
{
    x = x * 1;
}
func2()          /* multiply x by 2 */
{
    x = x * 2;
}
func3()          /* multiply x by 3 */
{
    x = x * 3;
}
```

In Figure 3.10, variable **x** is an external variable that is available to **func1()** and **func2()**. This variable is defined as being type **int** and declared to be "globally" available throughout the program in the same way that variables are global in a BASIC program, because the declaration of **x** comes before the rest of the program. The scope (or visibility) of **x**, therefore, is from the beginning to the end of the program.

In light of our discussion of the compile-link process, because **x** is defined outside the function, the compiler tells the linker that **x** is available to any function that needs it. Note that variable **x** is used in the **func1()**, **func2()**, and **func3()** functions, but that none of these functions has a declaration for **x**. (That is, an **int x;** declaration does not appear in any of the three functions.) The linker has no problem with this lack of declaration because the compiler told it that **x** is available to any function in the program. The scope of the external variable **x** is such that it is globally available throughout the program.

Note what this means: **x** is available to each function without the necessity of passing **x** as a function argument. Further, if **func1()** modifies the value of **x**, the new value of **x** will be available directly throughout the program; you don't have to use a **return(x)** in a function call. Enter the program in Figure 3.10 to verify this process.

There are other possibilities for external variables. C lets you write individual functions and save them on disk for inclusion in other programs through the linker. Consider the program presented in Figure 3.11, in which file 1 is the source program file, and file 2 contains a previously written function.

Figure 3.11

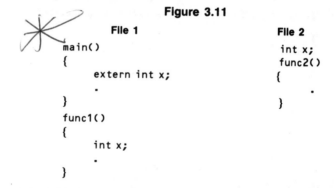

```
        File 1                          File 2
   main()                           int x;
   {                                func2()
        extern int x;               {
             .                           .
   }                                }
   func1()
   {
        int x;
             .
   }
```

In Figure 3.11, variable **x** in file 2 is an external variable because it is defined outside the function. File 2 can be linked with file 1 to form a complete program. *When two (or more) files are combined, however, the scope of an external variable will run from only the point of definition to the end of the file.*

If we want **main()** to have access to the external variable defined in file 2, we must use the **extern** declaration in **main()**. The **extern int x** declaration in **main()** causes the compiler to generate instructions to the linker to look outside file 1 for **x**. If we tried to use **x** in **main()** without any declaration for **x**, we would get an "undefined variable" error message from the compiler.

The **x** defined in **func1()** of Figure 3.11 is internal (and private) to the function **func1()**; its scope is limited to **func1()**. **x** is a variable totally different from those found elsewhere in the program. Whatever is done to **x** in **func1()** has no impact on any other **x** used in the program. Now study Figure 3.12.

Figure 3.12

```
              ⎧   main()
              ⎪   {                          extern int x;
              ⎪   }
              ⎪
File 1—  ⎨   func1()
              ⎪   {
              ⎪       int x;
              ⎩   }

              ⎧   int x;    /* Scope of x limited to file 2 */
              ⎪   func2()      /* unless extern elsewhere */
              ⎪   {
              ⎪   }
File 2—  ⎨
              ⎪   func3()
              ⎪   {
              ⎩   }

              ⎧   func4()
File 3—  ⎨   {
              ⎪       extern int x;
              ⎩   }
```

In Figure 3.12, if **main()** wants to use variable **x**, **x** must be declared in **main()** as **extern int x**. This declaration causes the compiler to generate instructions that allow the linker to find the external variable in file 2. Obviously, only one variable named **x** can be externally defined in a given program; otherwise, we would draw a "multiply defined variable" error from the compiler.

Any function in file 2 [i.e., **func2()** and **func3()**] can use the variable **x** without an **extern int x** declaration in the function because **x** was externally defined in file 2. The **x** is externally defined because it was defined before **func2()** and **func3()** were defined. By its placement in the file, **x** is externally defined to all functions located in file 2. When file 2 is compiled, the compiler makes **x** globally available to all functions in the file. The compilation of file 2 parallels the discussion of Figure 3.10.

The use of variable x in func4() must be declared. If it is declared extern int x, the external x from file 2 is used. When file 3 is compiled, the extern int x declaration causes the compiler to leave instructions for the linker to look outside file 3 to resolve the variable named x.

If a simple int x declaration appears in a function, it overrides the externally defined x from file 2. In Figure 3.12, func1() is one example of this process. Regardless of what func1() does to x, it will not alter the externally declared x in the program.

The scope of the external variable x in file 2 is limited to func2() through func3(). Either function can use x without any declaration of x. That is, func2() and func3() can use the external variable x without using an int x or extern int x declaration.

To make x visible in any other file requires the use of the extern int x declaration in any function that needs x. The compiler-linker's job is to find the external variable (assuming the programmer has done things correctly).

One final point is that typically the linker will automatically search the library to resolve any undefined variables or functions in the source file. If you have written and compiled a function, but not yet included it in the library file, most linkers allow you to specify files to be searched that are outside the library. Check your linker's documentation for details on how this is done.

Automatic Variables

The scope of an *automatic* variable is limited to the function in which it is declared. This means that the automatic storage class is the *default storage class* for C variables in a function. If a variable declared in a function has the same name as an external variable defined elsewhere in the same program, the automatic variable declaration will override the external variable. Automatic variables have values that are "local" to the function in which they are declared. That is, if x is declared in a function, we can change it as much as we want in the function without having any effect on the value of x used elsewhere in the program. The local values of automatic variables minimize the "side-effect bugs" mentioned earlier.

The program in Figure 3.13 illustrates how automatic variables work.

Figure 3.13

```
/* show the effect of automatic storage class variables */

main()
{
    int i, x;

    for(i = 1, x = 0; i < 10; i++, x++){
        printf("\n The value of x in main: %d", x);
        prove_it();
    }
}
prove_it()
{
    int x;

    printf(" The value of x in prove_it: %d", x);
}
```

In Figure 3.13, **x** is an (automatic) integer variable in both **main()** and **prove_it()**. Run the program above and look at what is printed. What happened? Why? What value for **x** was printed in **prove_it()**?

Remove the declaration of **x** in **prove_it()** and try to run the program again. Any problems? Now move the declaration of **x** in **main()** so that it is an external variable and run the program again. What effect did the change have? Why? Try removing the declaration of **x** in **prove_it()**. Any difference? You should experiment with a simple program like the one in Figure 3.13 until you are sure you understand both the distinction between external and automatic storage classes and their scope.

There is a great temptation for beginning C programmers to make all variables external. Resist the temptation, for it will only lead to trouble as program complexity grows. Scoped variables are a real asset once you get used to them, and they make program debugging and maintenance much easier.

Values and Scoped Variables

External variables retain whatever value they currently have through-out the program, or until they are assigned a new value in a function.

Automatic variables, on the other hand, "die" once the function is completed. Re-entering the function does *not* mean you can expect to find any variable in the function with the value it had when you left it. Indeed, C can just about guarantee that all variables will have garbage in them until they are assigned some value in the program. The value of **x** printed in the **prove_it()** function in Figure 3.13 will be whatever happened to be in memory at that location when the program was run (i.e., garbage).

Note: This also means that variables are *not* necessarily initialized to zero as in some BASICs. *External* and **static** variables are (sup-posed to be) initialized to zero by the compiler. *Automatic* and **reg-ister** variables are not. If you want a variable to be zero, it is best to assign it explicitly as such.

Although all of this may seem a burden, it does force you to be explicit about the initial values of variables. No doubt you've had bugs that were caused by not initializing a variable to the proper value. You will find this type of bug much less frequent in C.

static Variables

static variables can be either internal or external. If a variable is declared to be **static** in a function, it is local to that function like an automatic variable, but with one important difference: **static** *vari-ables remain "alive" even after a function is completed.* That is, whatever value was in the **static** variable the first time the function was completed will be in the **static** variable the next time the func-tion is called.

For example, to retain the value of **x** in the function **prove_it()** on subsequent calls, **x** would be declared:

```
static int x;
```

In this case, whatever value **x** has the first time **prove_it()** is exited will be the starting value of **x** the next time the function is called. (We are assuming that **x** is not initialized to some value in the function.)

An *external* **static** *variable* behaves in the manner that you might expect: it is available to only those functions defined in the same file in which the **static** variable is defined. In Figure 3.12 above, if **x** were defined as **static int x;** in file 2, only **func2()** and **func3()** would have access to it. An external **static** declaration, therefore, makes the variable available to those functions in the same file, but invisible to any other file. The scope of an external **static** variable is the file in which it is defined.

A function can also be declared as an *external* **static** *function*, which makes the function invisible outside its source file. This characteristic allows you to create a function in one file that will not conflict with another function outside that file, even when the two functions share the same name. We could, for example, make **func3()** unavailable to **func1()** and **func4()** by prefacing the function definition in file 2 as **static func3()**.

When a function needs to "pick up" where it left off the next time the function is called, internal **static** variables allow that operation without making variables external and, therefore, available elsewhere in the program. External **static** variables are useful when you want to limit the scope of an external variable to a particular file. **static** functions are afforded a degree of privacy they would not have otherwise. They also minimize the chance of collision with other functions that share the same name, but are defined in different files.

register Variables

register variables in C are normally used when execution speed is important. The idea behind the **register** storage class is to tell the compiler to reserve one of the CPU (Central Processing Unit) registers for a variable. Because data manipulation in a register is faster than in memory, execution speed is enhanced. Obviously, the **register** storage class is intended for variables that will be used extensively (e.g., loop counters).

For most microcomputers, the only declarations allowed for a **register** variable are **int** and **char**. Because the number of CPU registers in a microcomputer is limited, there is no guarantee that a register will actually be used. A good compiler, however, will try to use a CPU register for the variable if one is available.

Check your compiler's documentation to see if the **external**, **static**, and **register** storage classes are supported. (All compilers must support **automatic** variables.) Many C compilers implemented on microcomputers do not support the **static** and **register** storage classes. With the limited number of registers available in a microcomputer, there is no guarantee that a **register** variable will actually be used, even if it is supported.

Privacy and Functions

At the beginning of the chapter, we saw that an argument list gives the function the necessary data it needs to perform its task, and that the external storage class permits us to make variables available to a function without using an argument list.

But, what happens when an argument list is needed (i.e., we are ignoring the external storage class for the moment)? To illustrate this situation, suppose the following statements appear in **main()**:

```
int cub_num;

cub_num = 5;
```

Because **cub_num** is declared in **main()**, it is an automatic variable. Somewhere in memory an integer variable named **cub_num** is created and assigned the value of five. Let's assume that the compiler uses memory locations 20,000 and 20,001 to store **cub_num**, as suggested below:

Figure 3.14

20,000   20,001

0	5

What we have is the variable **cub_num** with a value of five that the compiler arbitrarily placed at memory locations 20,000 and 20,001. Now, let's say that we want to use **cub_num** in our **cube()** function, passing **cub_num** to **cube()**.

In **main()**, we might use the following line to print the cube of **cub_num**:

```
printf("The cube of %d is %d", cub_num, cube(cub_num));
```

which causes 5 and 125 to be displayed on the screen.

The function call **cube(cub_num)** is unique in C because when the **printf()** is executed, the call to **cube(cub_num)** creates a *temporary copy of* **cub_num** for use by the function. In other words, the compiler causes some variable, say **temp_1**, to be created and used in the call to **cube(cub_num)**. Where the copy is created is up to the compiler, but let's assume that it is at memory location 20,100. In memory, we would see:

Figure 3.15

For the function **main()**, cub_num resides in memory, starting at location 20,000. However, what the **cube()** function receives for **cub_num** is located at 20,100. In effect, it is as though the function call is actually **cube(temp_1)**. Both variables have the same value, but they are *not* the same variable. This is what is meant by the term *call by value*; the function receives a *copy* of the value, not the variable itself.

If this illustration is taken a step further, when the **return (cub_num)** in **cube(cub_num)** is executed, the relevant memory locations appear as

Figure 3.16

```
   20,000  20,001                    20,100  20,101
  +-----+-----+                    +-----+-----+
  |  0  |  5  |    .   .   .   .   |  0  | 125 |
  +-----+-----+                    +-----+-----+

  variable cub_num                 variable temp_1
```

In the `printf()` statement

```
printf("The cube of %d is %d", cub_num, cube(cub_num));
```

`cub_num` is printed with the value as it has remained in `main()`—that is, five. When `cube(cub_num)` is printed, `temp_1` is actually printed.

Functions receive copies of the value(s) passed to them. As a result, *a function cannot alter the value of the variable that appears in the function's argument list,* because the function receives a "call-by-value" copy of the argument, not the actual variable itself. This explains why variables are local to a function and not global like the variables in BASIC. There is a privacy in C that doesn't exist in BASIC, which is an advantage for the programmer.

At the risk of getting ahead of ourselves, how would you alter `cub_num` for further computations in the program? The astute reader has probably already figured out that all you have to do is give the function the *address* of where `cub_num` resides in memory and tell the compiler *not* to use a copy of `cub_num`. (This is easily done, and you'll see how in Chapter 4.)

Arrays: a Privacy Exception

An exception to the privacy rule on function calls occurs when an array variable is used in the argument list. An *array* is a grouping of similar data types that share a common name. A *character array*, for example, is an array of alphanumeric characters grouped together under one name. The two examples of array declarations shown below:

```
char message[10];
int num[10];
```

permit up to 10 different characters to be associated with the variable `message`, and 10 numbers to be referenced by the variable `num`.

To examine the first member of an array, use `message[0]` for the character array and `num[0]` for the integer array. Selecting a member of an array is much like subscripting in mathematics. The only difference is that *all arrays in C start with element zero*. Therefore, the fifth element in the character array is actually `message[4]`. (For those who aren't used to thinking about array element zero, just keep in mind that the one you want is one position lower than you might think!)

In C, arrays create an exception to the privacy rule discussed in the previous section. When an array variable is passed to a function, the function receives the location of the original array. Using the example above, if **cub_num** is an array that starts at memory location 20,000, **cube(cub_num)** receives the address of the **cub_num** array (i.e., 20,000) with instructions not to create a copy of the array. The function would receive the memory address of **cub_num[0]**, which means that functions can directly alter the data in any element of the array. This is true for both numeric and character arrays.

Why the exception for arrays? One reason for this exception is the manner in which a compiler handles arrays. Another reason is the need to conserve memory. Given that arrays tend to be large collections of data, whereas other (nonarray) variables are discrete units, duplicating arrays in function calls would tend to chew up large chunks of memory quickly.

Bear the distinction in mind: *Functions receive copies of all variables except numeric and character arrays.* Algorithms for programs in C should reflect this fact.

Designing a C Program

The variety of variable types and function calls in C gives a programmer a greater degree of control over the code than in BASIC. At the same time, this variety places some responsibility on the programmer to think through the code *before* it is written. The experienced programmer will begin writing a program with a block outline of what the program is to do. C allows you to write code in the same block structure, but much more easily than BASIC.

Suppose you want to expand the simple cube program to calculate the square of the number. Founded on the cube program, the outline of the new program might be:

1. Get the integer value to be squared and cubed.

2. Print its integer value.

3. Square the number.

Is it safe to square it?
a) If okay, square it.
   Return square to calling function.
b) If not, say it's too big and return zero.

4. Print the squared value.

5. Cube the number.
Is it safe to cube it?
a) If okay, cube it.
   Return cube to calling function.
b) If not, say it's too big and return zero.

6. Print the cubed value.

7. End of program.

Many programmers will take the outline and translate it into pseudocode. *Pseudocode* is an imaginary language that is essentially English with some of the programming language's syntax added. A pseudocode for our outline could be

Figure 3.17

```
main()
{
    declare working variables;

    initialize variable;
    print() its original value;
    call() and assign square; /* need a square function */
    print() its squared value;
    call() and assign cube; /* need a cube function */
    print() its cubed value;
}
```

The pseudocode should indicate any new functions you will need to write. It should also suggest what functions might be used from the C library (i.e., we need `printf()` again). You can then move to the functions you need and write the pseudocode for them. (Use the outline as a guide and try your hand at the pseudocode for the two needed functions.)

Pseudocode makes it easy to move on to the actual C code, presented in Figure 3.18.

Figure 3.18

```
/* take an integer and print its square and cube */

#define MAX_SQR 181   /* Number > 181 overflows square */
#define MAX_CUBE 32    /* Number => 32 overflows cube */

main()
{
     int i, x;

     x = 3;
     printf("\nThe value being used is %d", x);
     i = sq(x);
     printf("\nThe value squared is %d", i);
     i = cub(i,x);
     printf("\nThe value cubed is %d", i);
}

/*************************************************/
/* function squares integer, checking for overflow */
/*************************************************/

sq(i)
int i;
{
     if(i <= MAX_SQR)   /* MAX = 181 for squared integers */
          i = i * i;
     else {
          i = 0;
          printf("\nNumber too large for integer square.");
     }
     return(i);
}

/******************************************************/
/* function cubes integer, using square and original value */
/******************************************************/

cub(i, x)
int i, x;
{
     if(x < MAX_CUBE)    /* CMAX = 32 for cubed integers */
          i = i * x;
     else {
          i = 0;
          print f("\nNumber too large for integer cube.");
     }
     return(i);
}
```

The program begins with a simple comment that tells us what the program is designed to do. The #defines are used because they represent constants that may vary from one machine to another.

Integer variables use 16 bits on most systems. (This could change in the future.) If the number of bits does change, all you have to do to adapt to any new integer specification is change these two #define statements to the new values. You won't need to go looking through the entire program to locate and change the constants. Always use #defines when you work with constants that may be changed.

Note that #defines are substituted throughout the source program wherever they occur. Also note that they are declared outside any given function. In that sense, #defines behave the same way externals do: their substitution is available to all functions. Put another way, there is a "global" substitution of symbolic constants with #define.

The main() function should look quite straightforward to you. The cub() function is a little different in that we are passing two arguments to the function rather than one. (The function is called cub() to distinguish it from the earlier cube() function. In fact, we could have used the "cube" function, but purposely rewrote it to use two arguments.) A common mistake made by beginning C programmers is forgetting to declare the variables passed to the function. To repeat, arguments passed to a function must be declared after the function name, and before the opening brace of the function body.

Look at the statement used to call cub():

```
i = cub(i, x);
```

You can think of this statement as being processed by the compiler in a "right-to-left" fashion. That is, the compiler (1) gathers together the arguments i and x, (2) calls cub() with the copies of these variables, then (3) assigns the value returned from cub() to i. If you wanted to, you could accomplish the same operation with:

```
printf("\nThe value cubed is %d", cub(i, x));
```

As you saw in the original cube() function, arguments used in printf() can be functions. As far as the compiler is concerned, they work in much the same manner, except that the assignment of the value returned from **cub()** to **i** is no longer needed. If you plan to do some more work with the cubed value, assignment is necessary. Because **i** is an automatic (i.e., temporary) variable in **cub()**, its value disappears when the program returns from the function.

As an exercise, change the program so that it prints the answers in decimal, hex, and octal. Having done that, change the program so that one **printf()** function is used, but the **square** and **cube** functions are treated as arguments to **printf()**. This last change is not as easy as it first seems. (*Hint*: Keep in mind that we have "cascaded" the two functions. That is, we need the result of **sq()** before **cub()** can work properly. Think about it.)

Now that we have reviewed some of the details about functions, you may want to read again your compiler's documentation on each library function. With the exception of data types that we have not discussed yet, you should be able to understand what the function expects to be passed in an argument list, how these arguments must be declared, and what the function returns.

Try creating some of your own programs to use these functions. Having done that, design several functions of your own that may be useful to you. Do this until you have enough experience to be confident about using functions.

Chapter 4
Using Pointers in C

Pointers are the most confusing aspect of C for the beginner. Simply stated, *a pointer is a variable that points to another variable.* Pointers seem difficult at first because the average programmer has had little or no experience with them. Every computer language has pointers, but most languages don't allow the programmer to use pointers directly. C, however, makes them available to the programmer. They can be powerful tools once they are mastered.

To help you visualize how pointers work, let's consider how a hypothetical microcomputer memory system might look, as shown in Figure 4.1.

Figure 4.1

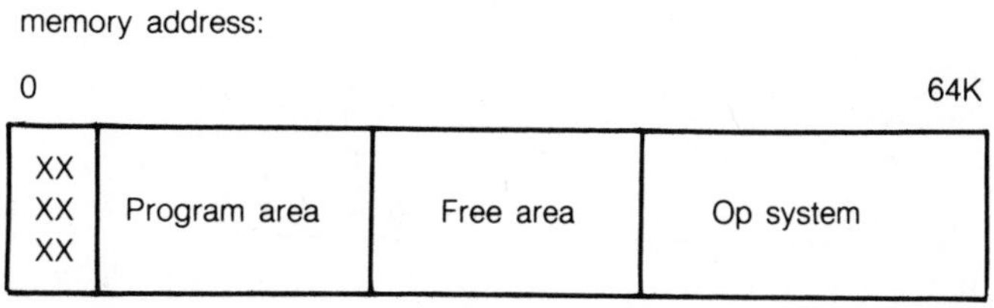

memory address:

0   64K

XX XX XX	Program area	Free area	Op system

A compiled C program occupies the lower segment of memory address space, followed by a free area for dynamic data storage (e.g., variables, constants, etc.). The operating system uses the higher memory addresses.

Let's assume that a program has the declarations

```
int number;
char letter;
```

in it. When the program is run, 16 bits (2 bytes) of memory are allocated somewhere in the free area for the integer variable **number** and 8 bits (1 byte) for the character variable **letter**. (This would be the allocation scheme for our hypothetical microcomputer, but may vary among machines.) Each variable is stored in a memory address in the free area.

To clarify this further, let's say that the variable **number** starts at location 15,000 in memory, and that **letter** is located at address 15,010. Let's also assume that **number** has been initialized to 3 and **letter** contains an ASCII x. These variables might be declared and initialized somewhere in the program as

```
int number;
char letter;

number = 3;
letter = 'x';
```

If we enlarge Figure 4.1 and use the values above, we should find the following:

Figure 4.2

memory address:

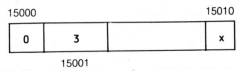

Whenever you use the variable **number** directly, the compiler must know *where* the variable begins (at address 15,000) and *how many* bytes (2) are required for storage. When you use **letter**, the compiler does not need to know *what* the letter is, but merely the *value* (15,010) for the letter's address and the *number* of bytes (1) required for storage. (Could this be one reason why all variables must be declared before they are used?)

A *pointer*, therefore, is a variable that *contains an address which points to some type of data.* Using our example, we can create pointer variables that point to the number **3** and the letter **x**. What we need to know now is how to declare and use pointer variables.

Declarations and Pointers

Thus far, we have used only the data types **int** and **char** in the sample programs and routines, a procedure that will continue until Chapter 6. There are other data types (e.g., **long int**, **float**, and **double**) that vary in the number of bytes required for storage. Pointers are also a type of variable, but they always use the same number of bytes (2 bytes for the 8-bit microcomputers).

The declaration of the pointer variable tells the compiler: (1) the address of the variable, (2) the number of bytes associated with the data type being declared, *and* (3) that the variable is to be used as a pointer.

An asterisk (*) must be used when a variable is declared as a pointer, as in Figure 4.3.

Figure 4.3

The declaration above tells the compiler the three things it needs to know about pointer variables: (1) I'm a pointer-type variable, (2) My name is **ptr_num**, and (3) I point to a type **int** variable. Until now, variable declarations conveyed only the data type and the variable name to the compiler. But now, the third item makes pointers different from other (nonpointer) declarations.

Pointers to characters behave in the same manner:

Figure 4.4

The declaration of a character pointer conveys the same three pieces of information as discussed above, except that a character pointer points to a character rather than an `int`.

Two more facts should be noted about pointers. First, because it is a memory address, a pointer always requires the same amount of storage regardless of the type of data to which it points. (For most microcomputers, two bytes are used for storing a pointer variable.) Second, a value of zero for a pointer is guaranteed not to point to valid data. This bit of information can be useful in many C programs. For example, if you call a function that is supposed to return a pointer, you can use a return value of zero to indicate that an error occurred in the function.

Initializing a Pointer

Before you can use a pointer, you must *initialize* it to point to something. A simple declaration of a pointer will not cause the pointer to point to anything useful. An uninitialized pointer will most likely point to some random (i.e., "garbage") place in addressable memory instead of where you want it to point. Therefore, *before* you use a pointer, be certain that you assign it a proper pointer address.

Suppose we want to initialize a pointer variable to point to **number**. We can do this with the unary **&** operator in C. The syntax is

```
ptr_num = &number;
```

What does **ptr_num** contain as its value? If we use the example presented earlier, **ptr_num** would have the value 15,000. The pointer variable **ptr_num** is initialized to hold the *memory address* where we can find the value of **number**.

A common mistake is to think that a pointer contains the *value* of a data type, but a pointer contains only an *address* that points to a data type.

lvalues and rvalues

Every data item in a language has an *lvalue* and an *rvalue*, which, if taken literally, mean *left value* and *right value*, respectively. In the example presented earlier, we created a variable **number** and initialized it with a value of **3**. We also saw that the compiler placed **number** in memory starting at address 15,000.

The *lvalue* (left value) of a data item is the address in memory *where* that item is located. For the variable **number**, the lvalue is **15,000.**

The *rvalue* (right value) of a data item represents *what* is stored at the data item's lvalue. In other words, the rvalue is what has been assigned to the data item. We can now visualize these two concepts as

Figure 4.5

Data Item

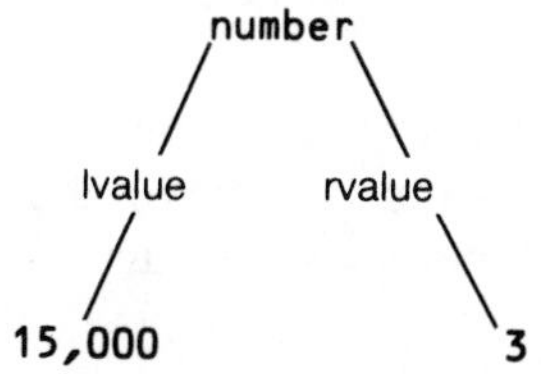

number

lvalue   rvalue

15,000   3

In this example, a data item **number** is stored at memory location **15,000** (its lvalue) and has been assigned the numeric value of **3** (its rvalue).

Now let's see how lvalues and rvalues relate to pointer variables.

lvalues, rvalues, and Pointers

Let's suppose that the following code appears in a program.

Figure 4.6

```
int number, *ptr_num;

number = 3;
ptr_num = &number;
```

Retaining the data from the example above, we'll assume that the compiler has placed **number** at memory location 15,000. Let's further assume that the compiler created the pointer variable (**ptr_num**) to reside in memory at location 16,000. Remember that the **&** operator assigns the *address* of **number** to **ptr_num**. The pointer **ptr_num** now points to **number**.

How do these assumptions relate to lvalues and rvalues? Consider Figure 4.7.

Figure 4.7

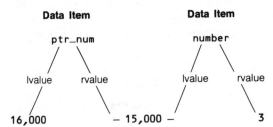

Note the relationship between the pointer variable **ptr_num** and the variable to which it points (i.e., **number**): the rvalue of **ptr_num** is the lvalue of **number**. Figure 4.8 displays this relationship another way.

Figure 4.8

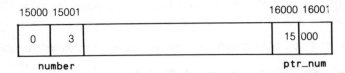

Now let's consider the compiler's point of view. It has two variables that can be used to access the same information. That is, the compiler knows: (1) that **number** is located at **15,000** (lvalue) with the contents of **3** (rvalue), and (2) that a pointer variable exists at **16,000** (lvalue) with the contents of **15,000** (rvalue).

Because the compiler knows that **ptr_num** is a pointer to **number**, the compiler can access the variable named **number** through a process called indirection. *Indirection is the process of accessing the* *contents of a variable (its rvalue) through its pointer variable, using the asterisk (*) operator.*

Consider the following lines of a C program for using pointers:

Figure 4.9

```
int number, *ptr_num, new_num;

number = 3;
ptr_num = &number;

new_num = *ptr_num;
```

Using the same numbers as before, let's inspect each line as viewed by the compiler. The first line declares two integer variables (**number** and **new_num**) plus a pointer to an **int** (**ptr_num**). The second line assigns the value **3** to **number**, and the third line initializes **ptr_num** to point to **number**. (This also means **ptr_num** has an lvalue of **16,000** and an rvalue of **15,000**.)

The fourth line shows the indirection process. The asterisk tells the compiler to (1) get the rvalue of **ptr_num**, 15,000; (2) get the integer contents stored at that location, **3**; and (3) assign the value found there to variable **new_num**. The variable **new_num** now contains the same value as the variable **number**, **3**.

The declaration of the pointer in the first line is important to the compiler. When you declare **ptr_num** to be a pointer to an integer, the compiler can then tell how many bytes to examine in retrieving what is stored. This declaration also tells the compiler that it can treat the rvalue of the pointer variable **ptr_num** (**15,000**) as a memory address. The asterisk in the fourth line simply tells the compiler to fetch the *contents* of the pointer variable's declared data type found at its (rvalue) memory address.

A few words of caution may prevent you from experiencing certain difficulties. First, you will create all kinds of trouble if you declare a pointer for an **int**, then try to use it to fetch a different data type. Worst of all, your program may appear to work if the compiler doesn't detect the error. Second, keep in mind that an uninitialized pointer will never point where you want it to point. Always initialize a pointer before using it. Try to visualize what would happen if these two rules were not followed.

The Importance of Pointers

You are probably wondering: "Why use pointers when I can simply make the assignment `new_num = number`?" Although you probably could make that assignment directly in the simple example above, there are two good reasons for using pointers.

First, a function cannot access directly a variable declared in another function. As we saw in Chapter 3, all variables (except externals) are local to the function. Whenever a function receives "outside" values as an argument list, the function receives copies of them (i.e., not the lvalue of the argument itself). So how can the programmer affect the original variable?

The only way to access a variable that "lives outside" a function is to use a pointer variable, which is part of the function's argument list. *A function must use a pointer variable in the function argument list for any nonlocal variable that is to be altered by the function.*

The only exceptions to this rule are external variables and arrays. External variables are an exception because they are "globally" available to all functions in the program. Arrays are an exception because they are not copied when they are passed to a function. (If you need to refresh your memory about this, review Chapter 3.) When arrays appear in an argument list, the function receives the lvalue of the array. In all other cases where pointers are not used, the function receives a copy of the variable.

Many beginning C programmers may be tempted to declare all variables as externals to simplify program writing. This practice gives rise to the *second* reason for using pointers: they minimize the "side-effect" bugs mentioned in the previous chapter. *One function cannot directly access a variable in another function.* When pointers are used to access variables indirectly, the risk of contaminating other variables in the program is reduced. C forces you to use indirection (i.e., with pointers) in a very deliberate manner whenever a function alters a variable outside itself.

Finally, keep in mind that if you call a function to alter the "original" value of a data item, you must use a pointer. If the function can perform its task simply by using a temporary copy of the variable, then you don't have to use a pointer. The only exception to this rule is an array variable. (If an array variable is used in the argument list of a function, the lvalue of the array is given to the function.)

Although pointers may seem difficult to understand now, it is well worth the effort to master them. You will appreciate them when program changes or debugging are required.

A Program Using Pointers

To test your understanding of how pointers work, let's write a program that (1) accepts a line of input from the keyboard, (2) asks the user to enter a character to be counted in the line of input, and (3) displays how many times the character occurs.

We'll need two new functions for this program: one to enter a line of text, and a second to count character occurrence. The rest of the program draws on elements we have used in previous programs.

Figure 4.10

```
#define MAXLEN 80              /* largest string size */

main()
{
    char string[MAXLEN+1], c;
    int count;

    printf("Enter a line of text.\n");
    getline(string);

    printf("\n\nEnter a character to be counted: ");
    c = getchar();

    cnt_let(string, c, &count);
    printf("\n\nThe letter %c occurs %d in the line.", c,
            count);

}
```

```
/* this function fills a character array until the RETURN key */
 /* is pressed, then adds the null to the end of the string */

char getline(s)
char s[];
{
     int i;

     for(i = 0; i < MAXLEN; i++) {
             s[i] = getchar();
             if(s[i] == '\n')
                     break;
     }
     if(i < MAXLEN)
                 ++i;
     s[i] = '\0';
}

/* this function receives the string (s), the character to */
 /* count in the string (which), and the address of where */
                 /* to store the count */

cnt_let(s, which, num)
char s[], which;
int *num;
{
     int i;
     *num = 0;
     i = 0;

     while(s[i] != '\0') {
             if(s[i] == which)
                 *num += 1;
             i++;
     }
}
```

What this program does first is define the symbolic constant **MAXLEN** for 80 characters. This symbolic constant is used in **main()** to set the character array variable named **string[]** to **MAXLEN** plus one. (Whenever we discuss an array variable, the variable name is followed by brackets.) One is added to **MAXLEN** so that we can add the character string terminator ('\0') to the end of the array. The **getline()** function limits the number of characters entered from the keyboard to **MAXLEN** (i.e., 80).

The program then asks you to enter a line of text and performs a

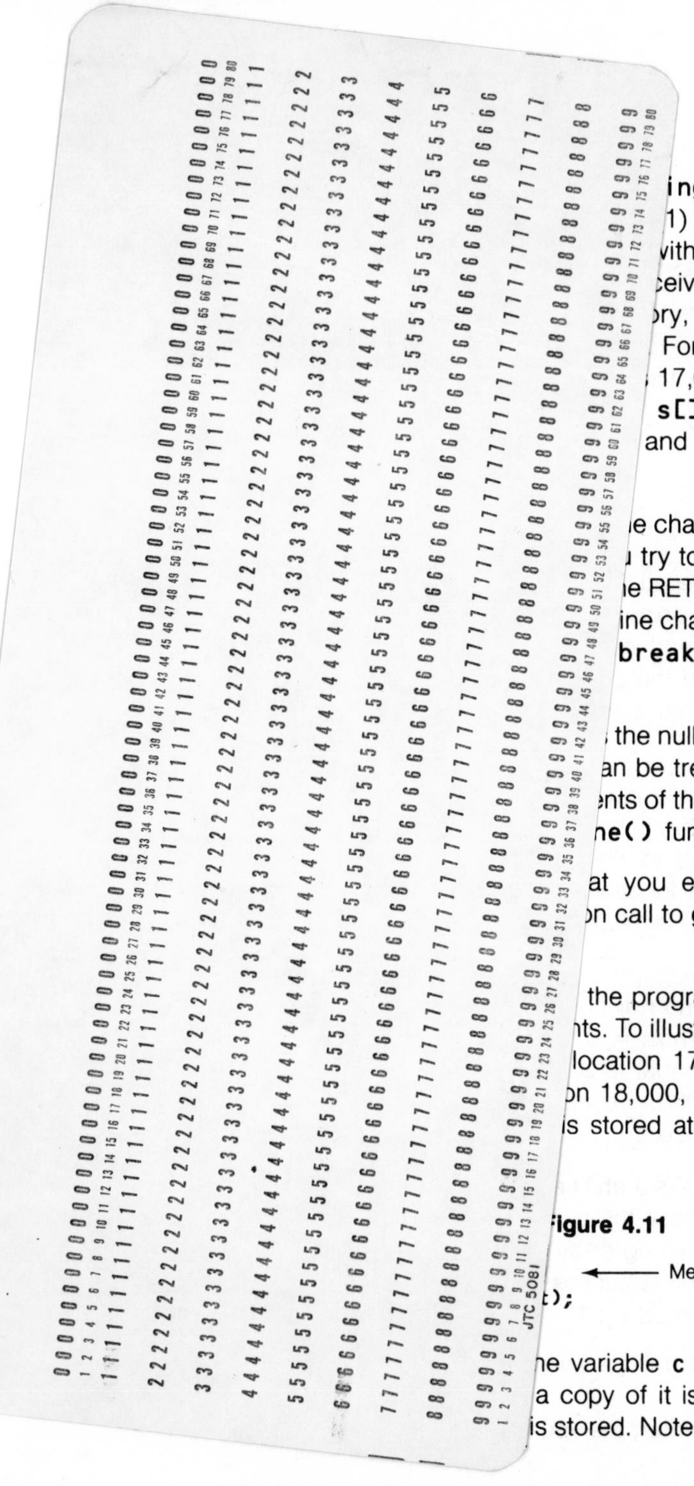

ing[] as its argument. There

1) the variable name **string**

without being referred to as

ceives the actual address of

ory, because character arrays

For example, if **string[]** is

17,000 (i.e., **string[0]** is at

s[] in **getline()**. The ad-

and s[0] in **getline()** are

e character at a time by function

try to enter more than 80 char-

e RETURN key, the program can

ine character ('\n'). The **if** state-

break statement throws you out

the null character ('\0') to the end

an be treated as a string. Because

nts of the array, there is no need to

ne() function call.

at you enter the character to be

n call to **getchar()** gets the char-

the program does a function call to

ts. To illustrate this, let's assume that

location 17,000, the character to be

on 18,000, and the number of occur-

is stored at location 19,000. We can

Figure 4.11

◄─────── Memory locations

t);

he variable **c** indicates that **c** is not an

a copy of it is sent to **cnt_let()**. We

is stored. Note that the program specifies

that the *address of* **count** (**&count**) be sent to the **cnt_let()** function.

If we look at this relationship from the function's point of view, **cnt_let()** sees it as

Figure 4.12

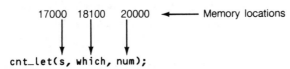

Because the argument declaration for variable **s** is a character array (**char s[]**), it is the same array as **string[]** in **main()** and has the same lvalue in **main()** and in **cnt_let()**. By the time we get to **cnt_let()**, the address of the copy of the character **c** in **main()** has been determined. (We've assumed that it is stored at location 18,100.)

The variable **num**, on the other hand, is an integer pointer to **count** in **main()**. The important thing about **num** is that it is a pointer variable with an rvalue that points to where **count** is located in memory. The lvalue of **num** (i.e., its location) is assumed to be at location 20,000. Its rvalue, however, is 19,000—the exact location of **count** in **main()**.

This program initializes **i** and **num** to zero in **cnt_let()**. However, because **num** is a pointer, ***num = 0** means that whatever value was at location 19,000 is now equal to zero. Because we know that the address of **count** is 19,000, we have set **count** to equal zero through the indirection process.

The **cnt_let()** function uses a **while** loop to test for the end of the character array. On each pass through the loop, a comparison between the character in the string array and the letter it is searching for (**c**) is made. If the search is successful, the contents of memory location 19,000 is incremented by 1.

```
*num += 1;      is the same as      *num = *num + 1;
```

Because we are using a pointer, the variable **count** from **main()** is actually being incremented each time the memory location is incremented.

Note: Whenever you want to use pointers to alter the contents of a number, you must use the asterisk in front of the variable name. This is why *num += 1; must be used in the cnt_let() function.

When the null ('\0') is read, the while loop terminates and control passes back to main(). Once again, no return is needed because we already have the number of successful comparisons stored in count. The program then prints out the results of the search and ends.

Enter this program into your computer and experiment with it. If your compiler supports the unsigned data type, try using the %u conversion character in printf() to print out the actual memory locations your compiler uses for count, num, s, and string[]. For example, you might have a statement in main() that appears as

```
printf("Address of count = %u", &count);
```

Then reread this section, substituting the actual values you found.

Another Example

To test further your understanding of pointers, study the program in Figure 4.13. Try to determine what should be displayed, then enter the program to see if you were correct.

Two functions [stuf() and mid()] are used in this program. The stuf() function fills a character array with the letters A-I. The mid() function prints a subset of the character array in the same manner that the MID$ statement works in many dialects of BASIC.

Figure 4.13

```
#define SIZ 9     /* maximum to look at */
main()
{
     int j;
     char letter[SIZ];

     stuf(letter);    /* fill array with characters */

     for(j = 0; j < SIZ; ++j)    /* print out the array */
          printf("%c ",letter[j]);

     printf("\n\n");

     mid(letter, 3, 3);
}

/* this function stuffs an array with letters A-I */

stuf(c)
char c[];
{
     int i, x;

     for(x = 65, i = 0; i < SIZ; ++x, ++i);
          c[i] = x;
}

/* this function prints the contents of a character    */
/*        array and is of the following form:          */
/* MID(string address, start of print, number to print) */

mid(p, start, num)
int start, num;
char p[];
{
     int i;

     for(i = 0; i < num; ++i)
          printf("%c",p[start + i]);
}
```

The program begins with a **#define** statement that sets the maximum size of the array (**SIZ**). Because 9 is the value assigned to the symbolic constant **SIZ**, the array has valid elements **letter[0]** through **letter[8]**. *All arrays in C start with element zero*, and the number of elements you "get" is determined by what you request in the array declaration. That is, the declaration

```
char letter[9];
```

requests nine elements in the `letter[]` array, not ten. It also follows that the first element is `letter[0]`, not `letter[1]` as in some BASICs.

The position of array elements follows an *N-1 Rule*. For example, the third element is actually `letter[2]`—that is, `letter[N-1]` = `letter[3-1]` = `letter[2]`. There is no default array size in C. (Unlike C, many BASICs default to ten elements without a DIM statement.)

The statement

```
stuf(letter);
```

calls the `stuf()` function to fill the array with the characters A-I. Note what has been done here. If we assume that the `letter[]` array resides at memory location 16,000 (i.e., the starting address of `letter[]`), we can visualize the call to the `stuf()` function as

Figure 4.14

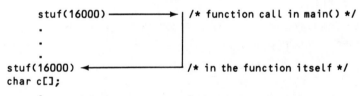

```
stuf(16000) ─────────────►  /* function call in main() */
     .
     .
     .
stuf(16000) ◄────────────┘  /* in the function itself */
char c[];
     .
```

The result of this call is that the `stuf()` function is passed the starting address of the `letter[]` array because arrays are not copied during function calls.

In the `for` loop, the **x** variable is initialized to the value 65, which corresponds to the ASCII letter A. The statement

```
c[i] = x;
```

says to take the value of **x** (which is 65) and place it in array element i of the **c** character array. Array element `c[0]` is, of course, found at memory location 16,000. Because of the initialization of **x** to 65 and the placement of x in i, the reference to c[0] on the first pass through the loop contains A.

On the second pass through the loop, x equals 66 (the ASCII letter B), and c[i] is now 16,001. This process continues for nine passes through the loop. When the loop is finished, memory addresses 16,000 through 16,008 contain the letters A-I. No **return** statement is needed in the function. Control automatically returns to **main()** when the closing brace of the **stuf()** function is reached. The program then resumes with the **for** loop in **main()**.

The **for** loop in **main()** prints out the contents of the array, with each letter separated by a blank space. Because **j** is initialized to zero in the loop, the contents of the array, starting with element **letter[0]**, are printed. The loop then prints out the remaining characters in the array. If we had added one more element to the **letter[]** array and placed a null in it, we could have used the **%s** conversion of **printf()** to print the array.

Remember that, as far as the compiler is concerned, it makes no difference whether you refer to the character array by name (i.e., **letter**) or by **&letter[0]**. Both are identical and yield the lvalue of the array.

Note: The lvalue of a variable is a constant. If **x** is a variable (not a pointer), we cannot say

```
&x = &x + 1;     /* Wrong ! */
```

because this line attempts to change the lvalue given by the compiler to the variable **x**. The compiler gets cranky if you attempt to change its placement of variables and will let you know it.

To return to the discussion, the program prints two *newlines*, or blank lines, by calls to the **printf()** function, then calls the **mid()** function with the following arguments:

```
mid(p, 3, 3);
```

in which **p** is a pointer to the beginning address of the character array, the variable **start** is the starting index of the array we want to print, and **num** is the number of array characters to be printed. These arguments can be visualized as

Figure 4.15

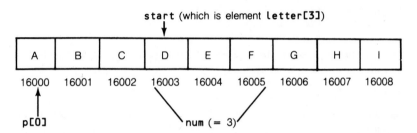

It is important to remember that when **start** equals three, we are asking for element **s[3]** of the array, *not* the third element. The two elements are not the same. (Refer to the N-1 Rule mentioned earlier.) If your program ever returns a list of data that is "off" by one, the chances are that you have forgotten about the zero array element.

Note the use of *p and p[]. When you *declare* a variable, there is no difference between *p and p[]; they are simply two different ways of declaring the same thing. When you are *using* a variable, if *p points to the beginning of the letter string, then it is the same as &letter[0].

The variable p[] has been declared as a pointer, so the statement

```
printf("%c", p[start + i]);
```

can be interpreted as

```
printf("%c", *p(16000 + i));
```

which prints the contents of memory location 16003, or the letter D. The **for** loop increments **i** until the three characters (i.e., **num = 3**) have been printed. Because there are no further statements in the **mid()** function, the closing brace sends control back to **main()**. Since no statements follow the call to the **mid()** function in **main()**, the program ends.

There is another test to consider: What happens if we change the **for** loop in the **mid()** function to read as follows?

Figure 4.16

```
for(i = start; num; i++, num--)
    printf("%c", ptr[i]);
```

Try to determine what will happen and then run the program with the modification. Are the results what you expected? More importantly, why or why not?

Although the program in Figure 4.13 is fairly trivial, it does point out one important aspect of the C language: if you need a statement that isn't provided in C, you can write a function to do it. Then you can place the new function in the "library" and use it in subsequent programs without having to rewrite it.

Incrementing and Decrementing Pointers

Pointer variables can be incremented and decremented like any other data type. Remember, however, that the increment/decrement operators function according to the data type being used. For example, suppose we declare an integer array of three elements and initialize the array with the values 1-3. Let's also suppose that the array begins at memory address 15,000 (its lvalue). This arrangement can be represented as

Figure 4.17

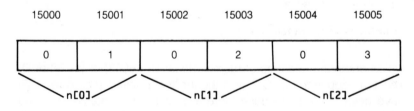

Because each integer requires two bytes for storage, when you increment a pointer to an integer variable, you actually increment the address held in the pointer variable by two. For example, if the variable **ptr** is a pointer to the **n** array, **ptr** will contain the address 15,000 after it is initialized. The statement

```
++ptr;
```

increases the address in **ptr** to 15,002 and makes **ptr** point to array element **n[1]**. The compiler automatically makes the necessary adjustment for you, provided that you have declared the pointer correctly. The variable **ptr** must have been declared as

```
int *ptr;
```

in the program prior to its use.

If we had mistakenly declared **ptr** as a character pointer, such as

```
char *ptr;
```

then used it to address the **n** integer array, the **++ptr** statement would only increment the pointer address by one byte rather than the two bytes needed to access the integer array. If a pointer points to a series of characters, the increment operation will add one to the address. The same operation on a pointer to a series of integers adds two to the pointer address. These rules also apply to the decrement operation on pointers.

Other data types may require between one and eight bytes for storage. (See Chapter 5.) The compiler must keep track of these requirements when pointers are used. The programmer must also make sure that the pointer actually points to the correct data type. If the pointer does not, then garbage data will creep into the program.

Look again at the library documentation that came with your C compiler, noting this time those functions that require pointer variables as part of the argument list. Try using several of those standard library functions in programs of your own. Pointers are a powerful feature of C when used correctly. If you practice using them now, your ability to use them efficiently will be well worth the effort.

Chapter 5
Input and Output in C

For those used to programming in BASIC, it may come as a surprise that C has no inherent input or output (i.e., I/O) statements. That is, C does not provide the equivalent of PRINT or INPUT as part of its syntax. How useful can a language be if it doesn't allow you to do any I/O?

Of course, C does allow for I/O in the form of function calls. One of its strengths is that you are not restricted to using predetermined I/O statements. In C, you can create whatever functions you need, or use the ones in the standard C library.

Using I/O Functions from the Standard Library

As discussed in Chapter 2, each C compiler has a number of *prewritten functions*. The `printf()` function, which we've used in most of our earlier sample programs, is one example. As you proceed through the book, you will be introduced to other functions that are usually part of the library.

The documentation provided with your compiler should describe the functions that comprise your library. Because the library is a collection of functions, the documentation should also explain what arguments are expected when each function is called. For example, the documentation might include:

```
int strlen(string)
char *string;
```

followed by a brief description of what the function does. In this example, **strlen( )** returns an **int**, which is the length of a character string pointed to by **string**.

The **strlen( )** function expects to receive a pointer variable named **string** that is a pointer to characters. The **int** before the function name tells us that this function returns an integer. (Is this label really needed? Recall that **chars** are promoted to **ints** in a function call.) The function description should tell us that the function returns an integer equal to the number of characters in the string. The length of the string does not include the null at the end. In other words, **strlen(x)** is the equivalent of LEN(X$) in BASIC.

Note that the description of the standard library functions is *permissive*, not *mandatory*. That is, you do not have to use a pointer named **string** for the function to work properly. For example, if the variable **c** is a string array:

Figure 5.1

```
main()
{
     int numchar;
     char c[];
     .              /* some statements that create the string */
     .
     numchar = strlen(c);
     printf("The length of the string is: %d", numchar);
     .              /* the rest of the program */
}
```

As suggested in the example, any variable name can be passed to **strlen( )** as long as it is a character array or pointer to characters; the variable does not have to be named **string**, as shown in the documentation.

After **strlen( )** is called from **main( )**, **strlen( )** returns an integer, which we have assigned to **numchar**. Variable **numchar** contains the number of characters in the string. We could also have done the function call as

```
printf("The length of the string is: %d", strlen(c));
```

and left out the assignment of the string length to **numchar**. Which use is better depends on how the string length will be used in your program. If you will need to use the string length in subsequent calculations, the first version is better because the string length is assigned to **numchar**. If you want to print the length of the string on the screen, the second version is more direct. Choose the version that is better for your program.

One final point about the standard library may be obvious to some, but not to others. If your program uses functions from the standard library, the actual code for those functions is supplied automatically by the compile-link process (see Chapter 6). That is, the C compiler supplies the code necessary for the standard library functions used in your program so that you do not have to rewrite them explicitly.

A Simple Program

Now that you know something about the standard library, let's use some of its functions to write a simple program to display your name on the screen.

Figure 5.2

```
#include "stdio.h"      /* read in the standard I/O file */
#define MAX 80          /* maximum length of name */
#define CLEAR "\014"    /* an ASCII 12 clears my screen */

main()
{
    char name[MAX];
    int c, i;

    printf(CLEAR);
    printf("Enter your name: ");

    for(i = 0; (c = getchar()) != '\n' && i < MAX-1; ++i)
        name[i] = c;

    name[i] = '\0';
    printf("\n\nYour name is: %s",name);
}
```

#include

Because most C programs use certain variables and functions, most C compilers have a *sublibrary* file that contains these variables and functions. You may want to think of the sublibrary as a file that contains *overhead* code for variables and functions that are used frequently in C programs. In Figure 5.2, the file that contains these functions is **stdio.h**.

The **#include** command is a *preprocessor* directive that instructs the C compiler to read the contents of a file into memory for use in the program. The command causes whatever is contained in that file to become part of the program (similar to the APPEND command in some BASICs). The general form of the **#include** directive is

```
#include "filename"
```

Note that the **#include** directive is not limited to a specific file. If you write a C program named **cursor.c** and want to include it as part of a new program, an **#include cursor.c** will have the same effect as rewriting **cursor.c** into the current program.

As you write more C programs, new programming tasks will often be reduced to selecting from work you've done in previous programs and **#include**-ing the selected files in the new program.

#define

The **#define** command establishes the symbolic constants used in the program (as discussed in Chapter 2). In Figure 5.2, **#define MAX 80** reserves 80 characters for the name and sets **CLEAR** to the ASCII code 12 (or 014 octal) that clears the terminal screen. Symbolic constants are used so that you can easily change these variables in the future. Otherwise, you would have to search through the entire program to find and change each occurrence of **80** and "\014".

Because "\014" is between quotation marks, it is a *string constant* that is stored in memory as '\014' and '\0'; the null is placed at the end of the string. A string constant is *not* the same as a character constant. A *character constant* appears between single quotation marks, e.g., '\014', and represents a *single* character; no null is added on.

String constants use the **%s** conversion character in **printf()**, whereas character constants use **%c**. A **%c** prints only one character at a time, but **%s** prints whatever number of characters is present before the null character constant ('\0') is read. (See the next section for details on the null character constant.)

If you have access to the source code for **stdio.h**, you should find a number of **#define**s there also. Whenever the compiler finds **MAX, CLEAR**, or any other **#define**s in the program, it substitutes the defined constants in their place. A **#define** results in a global substitution of the constants throughout the program.

Although the program in Figure 5.2 should look familiar to you by now, let's examine:

Figure 5.3

```
for(i = 0; (c = getchar()) != '\n' && i < MAX-1; ++i)
    name[i] = c;

name[i] = '\0';
```

In the **for** loop, the initial value of **i** is set to zero, and the terminal value of the **for** loop is a combined test of **i** and **c**. (**&&** is the logical AND operator in C.) The test on **i** is straightforward: we don't want more than 79 characters entered, because **MAX** was set to 80 by

#define. The 80th position (at most) must be saved for the null terminator.

The getchar() function, which is part of the standard library, gets a character from the standard input device (usually the keyboard). Because the documentation says that getchar() returns an integer, we have declared c to be an int. All characters in C are changed to an int in a function call. The getchar() function then assigns the character you enter to c. The character is tested in the for loop to determine whether it is (1) a *newline* character constant ('\n'), which corresponds to pressing the RETURN key; or (2) the 79th character. If neither condition is True, then the character is assigned to the proper element in the name[] array by the name[i] = c statement.

The for loop continues executing until either MAX-1 characters are entered or the newline ('\n') is detected. When either condition is sensed, the for loop is terminated.

This program line can be shortened. For example,

Figure 5.4

```
for(i = 0; (name[i] = getchar()) != '\n' && i < MAX-1; ++i)
        ;
name[--i] = '\0';
```

serves the same purpose, but fills the name[] array in the for loop construct itself. The characters returned from getchar() are assigned directly into name[]; c is no longer used. Don't forget the lone semicolon; it's a do-nothing statement, but needed by the for loop to function properly. This for loop is a common construct in C, so you should familiarize yourself with it.

The Null Terminator

After the name is completed, the name[i] = '\0' statement is executed. In the case of my name, the resulting string looks like:

```
Jack Purdum\0
```

In C, the '\0' character signals the end of the string. [The null character must be at the end of the string to tell strlen() that it has reached the end of the string and to inform printf() when to stop printing. Using this information, write your own version of **strlen()**, then compare it to the version in your library.]

The **printf()** function prints the string with the **%s** option. Because the null character has been added to the name, **printf()** properly displays the name as a string.

As stated earlier, the null terminator is a single character with a value of zero. More formally, an ASCII null has a value of *machine zero* (i.e., 00000000 in binary). We use the '**\0**' as a notation to signal that it is *not* the same as the ASCII *character* for zero. The decimal value for the zero ASCII character is 48 (binary 00110000), which is not the same as the null terminator (machine zero). Knowing the difference between the null terminator and the decimal value for zero is quite important. For example, instead of

```
.
while(*s != '\0')
.
```

we can use

```
.
while(*s)
.
```

because a **while** statement terminates whenever the test criterion evaluates to machine zero (i.e., False). Because the null character has a value of machine zero, we can leave out the explicit test for the null character. This reason for omitting '\0' may be difficult to grasp at first, but does make sense, and the omission occurs often in C programs. (Review the material in the Appendix to Chapter 2 if the concept seems unclear to you.)

Accumulating Functions

We can use the previous routine in a more general way than just entering it in a program. To that end, let's write a simple function to input a string from the keyboard, as shown in Figure 5.5.

Figure 5.5

```
/* a function that accepts a string from the keyboard */

inputs(s)
char s[];
{
     int i;

     for(i = 0; (s[i] = getchar()) != '\n' && i < MAX - 1; ++i)
          ;

     s[i] = '\0';
}
```

Let's assume that you save this routine (which is similar to Figure 5.2) on disk as **inputs.c**. You could then rewrite the program in Figure 5.2, as shown below.

Figure 5.6

```
#include "stdio.h"     /* read in the standard I/O file */
#define MAX 80         /* maximum length of name */
#define CLEAR "\014"   /* ASCII 12 clears my screen */
#include "inputs.c"    /* include the input string function */

main()
{
     char s[MAX];

     printf(CLEAR);
     printf("Enter your name: ");
     inputs(s);
     printf("\n\nYour name is: %s", s);
}
```

The program functions as it did in Figure 5.2, except that we did not write directly the **inputs()** function in the program. This time, the **inputs.c** was #**include**-d in the program and caused the compiler to include the **inputs()** code in the program.

The method used in Figure 5.6 to include the **inputs()** function is not the only way to get a function into a program. A better way is to make the function part of the standard library (after the function has been fully tested). The details of how to add new functions to the standard library vary, depending on the compiler you use. Your compiler's documentation should tell you how this is done. The compiled function can also be pulled in as a module during the link process.

Whether the new function is added to the library or linked as a discrete module, the advantage should be obvious. You can write a function once and make it available for use in other programs.

Debugging is also easier because you don't have to dig around in a program looking for each occurrence of the offending function. (Each program must be recompiled, however, after the function has been debugged.)

Some Details on String Arrays

We learned in Chapter 4 that array names are constants in C programs. When an array name is passed to a function, as shown in the **inputs(s)** statement in Figure 5.6, the function receives the starting address of the array. In other words, if **s[MAX]** starts at memory location 16,000, that is the address of **s[0]**. Once an array is declared, you cannot change its location in memory. It is a constant. You also cannot change (i.e., increment or decrement) an array name. Therefore, **++s** would be illegal because it attempts to change the *location* of the array in memory.

It is also true that the function call to **inputs(s)** passes the location where the **s** array starts in memory. The **input(s)** function, therefore, receives the starting address of the original array, not a copy of the array, as shown below in Figure 5.7.

Figure 5.7

```
inputs(16000)
char s[];
{
         .
}
```

However, because a pointer is a variable that points to the location in memory where another variable is stored, we can also write:

Figure 5.8

```
inputs(16000)
char *s;
{
        .
}
```

The result is the same for both versions: a pointer to the starting location of the **s** array (**s[0]**). Once we are in the **inputs(s)** function, the **char s[]** declaration will reference the starting address of the **s** array. Because the **char s[]** declaration references the starting address, the declaration behaves like a *pointer* that has been assigned to the starting value of the **s** array. As a result, you can also use a pointer declaration (***s**) with the same outcome.

If you look at the **inputs(s)** function in Figure 5.5, you will see that we didn't return anything from the function. Yet, the purpose of the function was to create a string from data entered at the keyboard. If **inputs(s)** did not receive the original location of the **s** array, we would not be able to use **printf()** in **main()** to display the name. Think about it.

Getting Numeric Data into a Program

When we created the function to enter a string from the keyboard, we relied on the standard library routine **getchar()** to do most of the work for us. This routine gets one character at a time from the keyboard. We can use the same concept for numeric data. C doesn't provide an input function for a number (i.e., there is no equivalent to INPUT A in C). You must write your own function (unless your compiler has one in the standard library). Figure 5.9 shows a crude version of the input function. (We have assumed that **inputs()** is now part of the standard library.)

Figure 5.9

```
#include "stdio.h"
#define MAXDIGIT 20          /* set max digits to 20 */

main()
{
    char s[MAX];
    int x;

    x = askint(s);
    printf("The number is: %d", x);
    printf("\nand its square is: %d", x * x);
}

/* this routine requests and converts a string to an int */

askint(s)
char s[];
{
    int i, sign, num;

    printf("Enter an integer number: ");
    inputs(s);               /* get the character digits */

    i = 0;
    sign = 1;

    if(s[i] == '-'){         /* determine if negative */
        sign = -1;           /* assume plus sign not entered */
        ++i;                 /* (we said it was crude!) */
    }

    for(num = 0; s[i] >= '0' && s[i] <= '9'; i++)
        num = 10 * num + s[i] - '0';

    return(num * sign);
}
```

The **askin()** function requests an integer number from the keyboard and relies on **inputs(s)** to create the string of digit characters. The **sign** is assumed to be positive for the number, but the **if**
statement checks to see if a negative **sign** were entered. If so, **sign**
is set to **-1**, and **i** is incremented to look at the next digit in the
string.

In the **for** loop, **num** is initialized to zero, and the character is
checked to determine whether it falls between an ASCII zero and

nine. If it does, the appropriate value is assigned to **num**. The routine ends by returning the product of **num** and its **sign**.

To illustrate how this program works, let's suppose that the character string contains "123\0" when it returns from **inputs(s)**. On the first pass through the loop, the '1' is translated as follows (using decimal values for the ASCII equivalents):

Figure 5.10

```
num = 10 * num + s[i] - '0';    /* s[i] = '1' */
num = 10 * 0 + 49 - 48;
num = 10 * 0 + 1;
num = 1
```

Subsequent passes through the loop find:

Figure 5.11

```
num = 10 * num + s[i] - '0';    /* s[i] = '2' */
num = 10 * 1 + 50 - 48;
num = 10 * 1 + 2;
num = 10 + 2;
num = 12;

num = 10 * num + s[i] - '0';    /* s[i] = '3' */
num = 10 * 12 + 51 - 48;
num = 10 * 12 + 3;
num = 120 + 3;
num = 123;
```

The loop then reads the fourth character, which is the terminator for the string. Because this character does not fall within the required range of values (it has a value of machine zero, remember?), the loop ends. In short, the scan of the string ends on the first nondigit, except the minus sign. The returned value is **123** because the **sign** variable has a value of plus one.

The **return** to **main()** displays the number, then squares it to prove that we are dealing with numeric values, not strings.

Most compilers have numeric conversion functions as part of the standard library. The **askint()** function is similar to the **atoi()** function found in most libraries, except that we prompted for the string as part of the function. The **atoi()** function (*ASCII to integer*) usually requests a pointer to the location of the string, then returns the integer.

Most libraries include conversion functions for every data type that is supported by the compiler. (Many compilers available for microcomputers do not support floating-point numbers, however.) The function **atof( )**, for example, converts an ASCII string to a floating-point number. Check your compiler's documentation for the conversion routines supplied in your standard library.

Output from a Program: printf() Options

Two other ways information can be displayed on the screen are **putchar(c)**, which displays a single character on the screen, and **puts(s)**, which displays string data only. Of additional alternatives, **printf( )** is preferred for its flexibility. However, **printf( )** is a complex function that generates a larger amount of code than **putchar( )** or **puts( )**. If you do not need the features of **printf( )**, then one of the alternatives should result in smaller program code size. As we saw in Chapter 1, the format for **printf( )** is

```
printf("control string", argument 1, argument 2, . . .);
```

The **control string** can contain the normal complement of ASCII characters plus the following special characters, or *escape sequences*:

Table 5.1

\n	=	newline (corresponds to a linefeed)
\t	=	tab
\b	=	backspace
\r	=	carriage return
\f	=	form feed
\0	=	null
\'	=	single quote
\\	=	backslash
\xxx	=	octal bit pattern

The **control string** may also contain a percent sign (%), which is a conversion character with the following available options:

Table 5.2

d	=	decimal
x	=	hexadecimal
o	=	octal (unsigned)
u	=	unsigned decimal
c	=	single character
s	=	string of characters (assumes \0 is the last character in the string)
e	=	decimal floating point in scientific notation (e.g., 1.234E11)
f	=	decimal floating point
g	=	the shorter of e or f

`printf()` also permits all of the above to be formatted as follows:

Table 5.3

-	=	left justification of the argument
	=	right justification of argument by default
l	=	el for the **long** data type (data types are discussed in Chapter 6)

Finally, the conversion character may be followed by a digit string (similar to that found in North Star BASIC and FORTRAN, but not too different from PRINT USING). If the leading digit is a zero, any blank elements in the field are filled with zeros. Some examples are shown below in Table 5.4. The broken vertical line represents the left side of the CRT. Let's assume that a string variable named **c** exists and contains the word "**computer\0**".

Table 5.4

Statement	Result
`printf("123456789012345");`	¦123456789012345
`printf("My name is:");`	¦My name is:
`printf("%s", c);`	¦computer
`printf("%-15s", c);`	¦computer
`printf("%15s", c)`	¦ computer
`printf("%4.2f", 123.456);`	¦123.46
`printf("%c", 'c');`	¦c
`printf("Answer is %d", 1234);`	¦Answer is 1234
`printf("x=%d and y=%d", 5, 8)`	¦x=5 and y=8
`printf("%05d", 17);`	¦00017

Experiment with each option until you are sure what effect it has on the resulting output. The `printf()` function is quite versatile, and you will find that it is capable of handling almost any output function.

scanf(), the General Input Function

So far, we have concentrated on functions that display the output of a C program. The `printf()` function has been the workhorse in most of the sample programs. The input side of I/O operations, however, gives a program the flexibility needed to make it useful in a variety of situations. (After all, who wants to recode-recompile a program each time a new set of numbers is used.)

We have used the `getchar()` function to get a character from the keyboard and do something with it in a program. This function, however, is a "low-level" means of entering data into a program. The `inputs()` function (Figure 5.5) used `getchar()` to construct an integer number in the `askint()` function (Figure 5.9). Despite these uses, a "high-level" input function that provides a more direct means of entering data would be very helpful. Such a function is `scanf()`, which is similar to `printf()` and has the same general format:

```
scanf("control string", argument 1, argument 2, . . .)
```

Because `scanf()` is used to enter data, the `control string` is used to specify the format in which the data is entered. The arguments to `scanf()` are supplied by the user (usually from the keyboard).

The `control string` may contain the same type of data as `printf()`. The percent sign (%) is used for conversion purposes, and the asterisk (*) has a special meaning that is discussed below. Table 5.5 contains an interpretation for the `control string`.

Table 5.5

```
d = a decimal integer
o = an octal integer
x = a hexadecimal integer
h = a data type of "short integer"
c = a single character
s = a character string
f = a floating-point number
```

Whenever **scanf( )** is used, the *arguments must be pointers* to the data type specified in the **control string**. For example:

```
scanf("Enter a number: %d", &num);
```

says we want a decimal number to be entered (the **%d** conversion), and the result placed in the variable named **num**. Because **&num** is used, the compiler places the number you enter at **num**'s address.

What happens if you enter a floating-point number instead of an integer? Usually the decimal fraction is stripped away. You should check the behavior of your version of **scanf( )** to see what happens. (It's a good idea to check all "standard" library functions to see what happens when unexpected data are entered.)

Some not-so-funny things can happen with **scanf( )** if you don't plan carefully. Consider

Figure 5.12

```
main()
{
        char adr[15];
        printf("Enter address: ");
        scanf("Enter address %s", adr);
        printf("Address is\n\n%s",adr);
}
```

Let's suppose that you enter "**123 Main Street**" for the address. You have entered an address with 15 characters in it, so everything is okay, right? Wrong! Don't forget that all strings must be terminated with a null (**\0**). Because the address uses all 15 characters of the array, there's no room for the null. You must make sure that the character array (i.e., **adr[]**) is large enough for the input *plus* the null terminator.

Another thing to keep in mind when you use **scanf( )** is that array names are pointers, so you should not use the ampersand (**&**) before such arrays in **scanf( )**. In all other cases, the arguments must be pointers to the data type requested as input.

When an asterisk (*****) is used in the control string for **scanf( )**, it becomes a special character that makes the program ignore the next data type you enter. For example, if

Figure 5.13

```
char name[15];
int num, new_num, old_num;

scanf(" %s %d %*d %d", name, &num, &new-num, &old_num);
```

receives

```
Fred 1111 2222 3333
```

from the keyboard, **name[]** receives **Fred**, **num** equals **1111**, **new_num** is ignored (because of the **%*d** in the control string), and **old_num** is **3333**.

If the control string is

```
scanf("%3d", &num);
```

and the input entered is **11111**, only the first three digits (i.e., **111**) are assigned to **num**. In other words, if a number follows the conversion character (**%**) and precedes the data type (**d**), it specifies the maximum width for the input field. The field width specification can be used with either numeric or string data.

The **scanf()** function should cover most types of input that you will need. However, you should verify that your "standard" library version of **scanf()** functions as it should. Indeed, we know of one compiler that does not supply a **scanf()** function in any form.

As an exercise, try writing C functions that duplicate the following BASIC input functions:

Figure 5.14

```
10 INPUT"Enter the address:", ADR
20 PRINT "Screen or Printer (S,P): ",
30 T$=INPUT$(1)\: REM Get only one character
```

Input Functions with a Little Class

Line 30 in the previous exercise asked you to simulate the INPUT$ (or INCHAR$) command found in most dialects of BASIC. Both of these input commands request that a single character be entered from the keyboard. These commands are often used when you must select from a limited choice where only a single keystroke is needed.

If you have ever used such commands, you know that they are usually preceded by some form of prompt to inform the user about what is being requested. A typical use in BASIC might be

Figure 5.15

```
100 PRINT "Output to Screen or Printer (S,P):",
110 T$ = INPUT$(1)
```

C does not limit you to a predetermined set of input routines. Because the prompt is usually needed, let's write a function that allows us to include the prompt as part of the input function.

Figure 5.16

```
main()
{
        char letter;

        letter = inchar("Enter a single letter");
        printf("\n\nThe letter is %c", letter);
}

/* this function requests a single character input */
     /* after printing a prompt on the screen */
inchar(prompt)
char *prompt;
{

        printf("\n%s",prompt);
        return(getchar());
}
```

The argument for the new **inchar()** function call is the prompt string that we want printed. This prompt string is passed to **inchar()** and displayed by **printf()** on the screen. The **getchar()** function allows a single character to be entered, which is passed back to **main()** through the **return(getchar())** statement. The program then displays the character that was just entered.

What would we do if we wanted a fixed number of characters to be entered, but not just one character? To do this, we need to add two new arguments to the program to determine: (1) the number of characters we want, and (2) a character array to store the input.

Figure 5.17

```
#define MAXLINE 80

main()
{
    char result[MAXLINE];

    inchar("Enter Zip Code .....\b\b\b\b\b", 5, result);
    printf("\n\nThe Zip is %s", result);
}

inchar(prompt, repet, answer)
char *prompt, answer[];
int repet;
{
    int j;

    printf("\n%s", prompt);

    for(j = 0; j < repet; ++j)
        answer[j] = getchar();
    answer[repet] = '\0';

}
```

The **inchar()** function in Figure 5.17 expands the argument list to include the number of characters wanted (**repet**) and a character array (**answer**) to hold the input.

Notice the backslashes (\b) used in the first **printf()**. Because a Zip Code has five digits (soon to be nine), we printed five dots to represent the field width. These dots give the user some idea of what is expected on input. The backslashes simply move the cursor back five spaces to the first dot in the field.

Because we want to treat the result as a string, the null character (\0) must be appended at the end of the input in the function.

We now have a generalized input function capable of printing various prompts and accepting any field width. The maximum length of the input string is limited to one less than the symbolic constant

MAXLINE. (It must be one less so that we can append the null at the end.)

To test your understanding, try modifying the **inchar()** function so that the letters are not displayed on the screen as they are entered. (This might be useful for entering a password in a program. *Hint*: Try a symbolic string constant **BACKERA " \010"**. Note the blank space before the backslash.)

A Little More Class

Most CRTs let you position the cursor at any given row-column coordinates on the screen. We can do this in C by using direct cursor control. Before you can use direct cursor control in a program, you must know the appropriate CRT codes. The control codes for several popular CRTs are listed in Table 5.6.

Table 5.6

Direct Cursor Control and Clear Screen Codes

CRT Screen	Cursor Codes	Clear
ADM-3	27, 61, -1, 31	26
ADDS, Intertec	27, 89, 31, 31	12
Advantage	27, 62, 31, 31	30, 15
Hazeltine	126, 17, -1, -1	126, 28
Heath, Zenith	27, 89, 31, 31	27, 69
Infoton	27, 102, 31, 32	12
OS1	27, 61, 32, 32	26
SOL	27, 2, -1, 27, 1, -1	11
Soroc, Televideo	27, 61, 31, 31	27, 42
SWTP	11, -1, 1	28, 18

The codes in Table 5.6 are (ASCII) decimal values. Typically, such constants in a C program are written as an escape sequence in octal, or base eight, numbers. The escape sequence for decimal 27 is '\033'. (The second digit times 8 plus the third digit = 8 times 3 plus 3 = 27. For decimal 20, it is '\024' in octal.)

If you look in the table, the cursor codes for the ADDS, Zenith, and Heath terminals are the same. Because the decimal number for 89 in the ASCII character set is 'Y', we can write the sequence as

"\033Y". Quotation marks are used because two characters are needed. (Single quotation marks are used for single characters, not a sequence of two or more characters.)

You cannot use a decimal 27 for the ASCII Escape because decimal 27 is not a printing character in ASCII. (If you tried "27Y", that's exactly what you would see on the screen when it is printed. The Escape code 27 gives the CRT the information it needs to initiate special functions for the terminal.)

Because you may want to start the program with a clear screen, the clear screen codes are included in Table 5.6 for each CRT. If your particular CRT is not on the list, you should be able to find the proper codes in your CRT manual. Try looking under "direct cursor addressing," "loading the cursor," and "clear screen-home cursor."

The program in Figure 5.18 illustrates one use of direct cursor control. Take a few minutes to study the program, then key it into your computer. (See page 112.)

Figure 5.18

```
#define CLEARS    '\014'      /* Clears screen for my CRT */
                              /*    and is a decimal 12    */
#define CURSPOS  "\033Y"      /* Cursor control lead in    */
                              /* 27 and then 89 = Y in     */
                              /*           ASCII           */
#define BELL      '\007'      /*    CRT ASCII bell code     */

main()
{
        char letter;
        int er;

        er = 0;
        putchar(CLEARS);
miss:   set_curs(5, 15, 0);
        letter = inchar("Enter a digit 0 through 9");
        if(letter < '0' || letter > '9'){
                er = set_curs(1, 50, 1);
                goto miss;
        } else
                puts("\nEntry was a digit");
        if(er == 2)
                set_curs(1, 50, 2);
}

/* this function positions cursor at the row-column */
/* coordinates given by function call. If ring */
/* variable is 0, normal cursor control done. If */
/* ring is 1, bell sounded. Any other value, the */
/* previous error message is erased. */

set_curs(row, col, ring)
int row, col, ring;
{
        printf("%s%c%c", CURSPOS, row + 31, col + 31);
        if(ring == 0)
                return (0);
        if(ring == 1){
                ring = 2;
                puts("ERROR");
                putchar(BELL);
                return(ring);
        } else
                puts("                              ");
}               return (0);
```

```
inchar(prompt)
char *prompt;
{
        char c;
        printf("\n%s: ",prompt);
        c = getchar();
        return(c);
}
```

This program uses the **inchar()** function discussed earlier to enter a single digit from the keyboard. Note the use of the words **miss** and **goto miss** in the program. The former is a label that references a specific statement in the program. The **goto** followed by a label reference transfers program control to the statement following the label name-colon. The general form is

```
label_name :
goto label_name;
```

The colon must follow **label_name**.

When we first reach **miss**, we set the cursor at row 5, column 15, and call the cursor positioning function **set_curs()**. The row-column coordinates tell the function where to print the prompt on the screen.

The function call to **set_curs()** also passes a third argument to the function to detect an error condition. When the function is first called, the variable named **ring** is set to zero. When **set_curs()** receives its arguments, it positions the cursor at row 5, column 15. Because **ring** has a value of zero, the **if** statement causes a **return (0)** to **main()**.

The program then calls **inchar()** to get a character from the keyboard. The **if** statement in **main()** checks to see if a digit was in fact entered. If it was not, then **set_curs()** is called again, but with different arguments. Now the row-column coordinates are used to print an error message in an *error window* located at row one, column 50. Because **ring** equals one on entering the function, the **if** statement in **set_curs()** reassigns **ring** to equal 2, prints the error message in the window, and rings the CRT's bell.

Note that the variable **er** is assigned the value of **ring** when it is returned from **set_curs()**. If an error occurred, you should try to prove to yourself that **er** now equals 2.

When control returns to **main()**, the **goto miss** is executed. The **goto** statement causes control to be sent unconditionally to the location of the label name after the **goto**. In our example, control is sent to **miss**. Program execution resumes with the statement that follows the label name. The program then asks you to re-enter the character.

This time, if a digit is entered in **main()**, the program will print a message to indicate that a digit was entered. If an error was made, the error message ("**ERROR**") is still on the screen in the error window. Because everything is okay now, we need to "erase" the error message. This is exactly what the final call to **set_curs()** does in **main()**. It prints 28 blank spaces in the error window, which erases the word **ERROR** from the screen. The **if** statement in **main()** assures that the final call to **set_curs()** will be performed only if an error message is on the screen.

In Figure 5.18, **printf()** and **puts()** were used to print information on the screen. The two functions do have similar uses. **printf()** is the formatted print function. **puts()** writes (puts) a string on the screen, as shown below.

```
puts(string)
char *string;
```

There are two basic differences between **printf()** and **puts()**. First, **printf()** can use one or more arguments, the first being the control string; whereas **puts()** has only one argument, the string (character array) to be put to the screen. This means that **printf()** will perform formatting functions (**%6.2f**, **%s**, **%-6.d**) when printing, but **puts()** does not perform any formatting conversions. If you need formatted printing, you must use **printf()**. However, both **puts()** and **printf()** recognize and properly translate all escape characters (\r for carriage return, \b for backspace, \t for tab, etc.).

The second difference varies between compilers, and you should verify this with your compiler's documentation. **puts()** automatically prints a newline (\n) after the string is printed, but **printf()** does not. This means that the cursor automatically advances to the first position of the next line after printing the **puts()** string. With the **printf()** function, the newline character must be included in the control string. For example,

```
printf("%s\n",
       "The cursor moves to the next line after the period");
```

puts() executes faster and is easier to use than **printf()**. The newline (\n) character is automatically printed at the end of the string. **printf()** is more versatile. To simply write a string of characters to the screen, either **puts()** or **printf()** may be used. If the cursor should not advance to the next line (as we did with the **inchar()** function) or if formatted printing is required, use **printf()**.

The switch() Statement

Let's take another look at the **set_curs()** function. Once the cursor is positioned at the desired location, we have a series of **if** statements that depend on the value of **ring**. This series can be written in BASIC as

Figure 5.19

```
100 IF RING>1 THEN RING=2 ELSE RING=RING+1
110 ON RING GOTO 120,130,140
120 RETURN
130 RING=2:PRINT "ERROR" CHR$(7):RETURN
140 PRINT "                              ":RETURN
```

C provides a similar alternative to the BASIC ON-GOTO, which is also used to replace a series of **if** statements. Let's rewrite the BASIC program as

Figure 5.20

```
set_curs(row, col, ring)
int row, col, ring;
{
        printf("%s%c%c", CURSPOS, row + 31, col + 31);
        switch (ring) {
          case 0:
                return (0);
          case 1:
                ring = 2;
                puts("ERROR");
                putc(BELL);
                return(ring);
          default:
                puts("                              ");
                return (0);
        }
}
```

The **set_curs()** function performs as before, but uses the **switch** statement to decide which **case** to execute. The **switch** is followed by an integer expression that determines which **case** will be executed. In Figure 5.20, the value of **ring** is used, then compared with the expression that follows **case**. If a match is found (e.g., **ring = 0** is **case 0**), then the program statements for that **case** are executed.

The **default case** is just that: If there is no match between the **switch** expression and a **case**, the **default** is executed. If the **default case** is left out and there is no match, no **case** is executed.

If you are in a **case** in a **switch** and want to exit the **switch** when you are done, use a **break** statement. A **break** statement causes control to exit from a **switch** in much the same way it does in a loop.

Note that each **case** must evaluate to a constant integer expression and be followed by a colon. Modify the program to include the form in Figure 5.20 and experiment with it. One possibility is to have different **cases** for different error messages and to use the value of **ring** to select the appropriate one. This way, you can get more informative messages than just **"ERROR"**. Give it a try.

Chapter 6
Other Data Types

Until now, we have used only character and integer variables. Most C compilers, even the most inexpensive, support these two data types. However, many applications require floating-point numbers (i.e., numbers with a decimal fraction) or integers with values that exceed the limits of those used thus far.

If your compiler doesn't offer data types other than `int` and `char`, you should still read the rest of this text. The fact that you've made it this far suggests that you have more than a passing interest in C, and you may want to upgrade to a more complete C compiler. Appendix B can help you make a selection.

Fundamental Data Types

C has four basic data types:

```
char        int        float        double
```

We already know about the `char` and `int` data types, including their storage requirements and range. A `float` data type represents a single-precision, floating-point number (i.e., a number with a decimal value like 3.14). A `float` typically is stored as a 32-bit number with 6 digits of precision.

117

A **double** data type represents a double-precision, floating-point number. Usually, a **double** has 14 digits of precision and is stored internally as a 64-bit number. **doubles** represent the same type of data as a **float**, but do so with greater precision.

Why settle for less than **double**? First of all, a **double** requires twice as much storage as a **float**. Second, a variable often doesn't need to be either a **float** or a **double**. A variable that controls a **for** loop is a common example. Because integer numbers contain fewer bits, they are processed faster than **floats** or **doubles**. The programmer must decide which data type is best for a given situation.

Keep in mind that the exact precision and internal bit requirements for each data type may vary among machines. Each C compiler can be written with different design goals and hardware restrictions. For example, most microcomputers use an 8-bit data bus, and data types tend to be even multiples of 8 bits. With the increased popularity of 16-bit machines, some data types may change bit requirements.

It's important not to jump to conclusions about precision and bit requirements. Even if the bit requirements are the same for each data type, the numeric precision may vary because of the way numbers are processed internally. Other things being equal, arithmetic processing in binary is faster than Binary Coded Decimal (BCD). However, binary arithmetic is more prone to rounding errors for a given bit representation than BCD. Such differences may be unimportant in counting cell growth, but are critical in accounting applications. Check your compiler's documentation for details about how the data types are processed.

Extensions of the Fundamental Data Types

Other data types can be derived from the four data types mentioned above. In C, the words **long**, **short**, and **unsigned** can be used as adjectives to create new data types. The following line illustrates how these new data types are formed:

```
short int,    unsigned int,    long int,    long float
```

short

A **short int** is an integer number that can be positive or negative. Although the creators of C probably intended **short int** to be an integer that was smaller than an **int**, on most computers it is identical to an **int**. (An exception could be larger computer systems.) Check your compiler's documentation to see if there is any distinction.

unsigned

An **unsigned int** is an integer number that assumes only positive values. Because an **unsigned int** is not sign extended, it can assume larger values than an **int**. For most micro- and minicomputers, an **unsigned int** uses 16 bits and has a value between 0 and 65,536 (i.e., 2^{16}).

If you tried to print a pointer address with the **%d** conversion character in any of the sample programs, the pointer address was probably displayed as a negative number. This happened because data addresses are often stored in high memory—addresses that exceed the permitted range of an **int**. If you use the **unsigned** conversion character (**%u**) in **printf()**, the correct address will be displayed.

long

The adjective **long** can be used with either integer (**long int**) or floating-point (**long float**) numbers. A **long** varies among systems, but its bit requirements are usually *twice* that of an **int**. For micro- and minicomputers, a **long int** requires 32 bits and may assume positive or negative values. Permissible values for a **long int** range from $-2,147,483,648$ to $2,147,483,647$—a fairly large range.

A **long float** has twice the bit requirement of a **float**, which makes it the same as a **double**. Therefore, there is no distinction between a **long float** and a **double**, and a **long float** is treated as a **double** by the compiler.

Whenever an adjective (**short**, **long**, or **unsigned**) is used without a data type specifier, the compiler treats it as an **int**. For example,

```
unsigned address;
```

```
short steps;
long walk;
```

results in the compiler treating the variables as **ints** (i.e., **long int address**, **short int steps**, and **long int walk**). If you use an adjective without a data type specifier, the variable will default to its **int** data type.

Mixing Data Types

With all of the data type options available, you might think that confusion would reign supreme when arithmetic operations are performed. In fact, they are performed in an orderly manner, with the compiler taking care of most of the details. The rules for these operations are discussed below.

char and int

Rule 1. Any variable of data type **char** that is used in an arithmetic expression is converted to an **int**. For example, the **atoi(string)** function in C has the same purpose as the VAL(S$) statement in BASIC: it converts an ASCII string of character digits to an integer. If you examine the code for **atoi()** in the library, you will see one line of code in the function that looks similar to

```
number = 10 * number + string[i] - '0';
```

Remember that a character data type can be used in an arithmetic operation. To do this, the compiler first promotes (automatically) the character to an **int**. In this case, **string[i]** and the character constant **'0'** are both converted to an **int** before the arithmetic operations (multiply, add) are performed.

Conversion and Assignment

Rule 2. Whenever different data types are used in an assignment expression, the data type on the right side of the expression is converted to the one on the left side. Consider

```
number = string[1];
string[2] = number + 1;
```

In the first case, **string[1]** is converted to an integer, then assigned to **number**. Because a character data type needs fewer bits than an **int**, **string[1]** is normally zero-filled on the left during conversion. (The designer of the compiler has some latitude on this.)

In the second case where an integer is assigned to a character, any excess bits in **number** are thrown away before the assignment to **string[2]**. Because **chars** are typically 8 bits and integers 16 bits, the "top" (i.e., most significant) 8 bits of **number** are discarded.

Type conversions are also performed on other data types during assignment. If, as in Figure 6.1, there is

Figure 6.1

```
float big_num;
int little_num;

little_num = big_num;
```

then **float big_num** is forced to an integer before the assignment to **little_num**. If **big_num** contains a decimal fraction, it is truncated to an integer before assignment. If the process involves moving from **double** to **float**, rounding is performed (not truncation).

Binary Operators and Mixed Data Types

Rule 3. A *binary* operator needs two operands. For example, when you multiply 2 times 3, the numbers 2 and 3 are the operands. Multiplication, therefore, is a binary operator because two operands (i.e., numbers) are required. Likewise, addition, subtraction, and division are binary operators. A *unary* operator has one operand, and a *ternary* operator needs three operands.

If you perform a binary operation (two operands) on two different data types, the compiler will convert the smaller operand to the "higher" data type. A higher data type requires the greatest number of bits for internal storage. If an **int** and a **double** are multiplied, for example, the **int** will be forced to a **double** before multiplication because the **double** has a higher bit requirement. The result becomes the higher data type—a **double** in this example.

Floating-Point Arithmetic and Double Precision

Rule 4. If two floating-point numbers are used in an arithmetic expression, both will be promoted to **double** before the arithmetic operation is performed. If the result is assigned to a **float**, it is *rounded* to fit the **float**. If the result is assigned to an integer, it is *truncated* to fit the (smaller) **int**.

Function Arguments and Promotion

Rule 5. If a **char** or **short** is passed to a function as part of an argument list, both will be promoted to an **int**. Likewise, a **float** is promoted to a **double**. However, **is_letr** may be used as type **char**, and **is_flot** may be used as a **float** in the function. This might appear as

Figure 6.2

```
main()
{
      char is_letr;
      float is_flot;
      .
      .
      dummy(is_letr, is_flot);
      .
      .

}

dummy(let, flot)
char let;
float flot;
{
      .
      .
      .
}
```

The **char** and **float** in **main()** are promoted to an **int** and a **double** when passed to **dummy()**. However, they are declared as **char** and **float** in the argument declarations.

Promoting the Unpromoted

Despite the five rules above, there are operations where the data types are not changed automatically. What do you do when you want to change a data type, but the compiler won't do it automatically for you? For example, let's suppose that you have two variables: one an **int**, and the other a **double**. Normally, both numbers would be promoted to a **double** before an arithmetic operation (see Rule 3). But let's suppose that you want the result to be an **int**. In this case, you would use a **cast**.

A **cast** in C *lets you convert one data type into another*. This means that you can force a conversion of data types and "unpromote" a data type that normally is promoted by the compiler. A **cast** has the form

    (data type) expression

in which the data type to **cast** is the data type you want. If you wanted to divide **dbl_num** by **int_num**, then the result would normally be a **double**. By using a **cast**, however, you can unpromote the **double** to an **int** after division. The syntax is

Figure 6.3

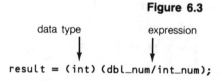

By using a **cast**, you force **dbl_num** to an **int** after the integer division is performed. The answer assigned to **result** is an **int**. If you did not use **cast**, the **result** would be a **double**. If **result** is an **int** and no **cast** is used, most compilers would generate an error message.

Using Other Data Types

We can use the information above to write a square root function for your library. We shall assume that the number is entered from the keyboard and stored internally as a string. Therefore, we will need first a function to convert the string of character digits to a floating-point number, then a function to determine the square root of the number.

Let's examine the function to convert ASCII characters to a floating-point number.

Converting ASCII Characters to a Floating-Point Number

Consider Figure 6.4.

Figure 6.4

```
/* converts character string to floating-point number */
double atof(s)
char s[];
{
     double val, power;
     int i, sign;

     i = 0;
     sign = 1;
     if(s[i] == '+' || s[i] == '-')
          sign = (s[i++] == '+') ? 1 : -1;
     for(val = 0; s[i] >= '0' && s[i] <= '9'; i++)
          val = 10 * val + s[i] - '0';
     if(s[i] == '.')
          i++;
     for(power = 1; s[i] >= '0' && s[i] <= '9'; i++){
          val = 10 * val + s[i] - '0';
          power *= 10;
     }
     return(sign * val / power);
}
```

The function begins with a type specifier which states that the function named **atof()** returns a **double** from the function. The argument supplied to the function is declared to be a character array. The character array holds the character digits to be converted.

The body of the function sets up some temporary variables, then checks to see if the first digit in the array is a plus or minus sign. If a plus or minus sign is present, the line

```
sign = (s[i++] == '+') ? 1 : -1;
```

is executed. This line is an example of a *ternary operator* with the general form

express 1   ?   express 2   :   express 3**;**

The ternary operator agrees with what we stated earlier: it requires three operands. If expression 1 evaluates to logic True, then expression 2 is evaluated. If expression 1 is logic False, then expression 3 is evaluated. This process can be illustrated as

Figure 6.5

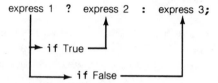

The ternary operator is similar to IF-THEN-ELSE in BASIC. The BASIC and C equivalents of the above might be

Figure 6.6

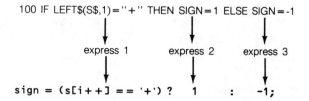

The ternary operator in C replaces the simple IF-THEN-ELSE conditional expression in the BASIC program line. This line could be rewritten in C without the ternary operator as

Figure 6.7

```
if(s[1] == '+')
      sign = 1;
else
      sign = -1;
```

Once you become accustomed to seeing the ternary operator, it provides a more concise and readable way of stating simple **if-else** statements.

After the **sign** is determined, the function uses the digits in the string to construct the number. Notice that we have used Rule 3 to construct the number. Each digit is a **char** in the array, but is promoted to a **double** because of Rule 3: operands in arithmetic functions are elevated to the highest operand used in the expression. Because we are using the variable **val** as a **double**, all operands in the expression become a **double**. That is, the result of **s[i]-'0'** is promoted to a **double** before it is added to **val**.

If the character string contains a decimal point, **i** is incremented to pass over it and read the decimal fraction. Each character read after the decimal causes power to be multiplied by ten, which is necessary because of the way **val** is calculated. For example, if the character string entered is **4.12**, **val** equals **412** just before the **return()** is executed. Because power equals 100, however, the **return** statement becomes

```
return( 1 * 412 / 100);
```

and returns the proper value of **4.12** from the function. Bear in mind that the value returned is a **double**. (Rule 5. The function is also explicitly declared to return a **double**.)

The **atof()** function in Figure 6.4 is fairly crude (e.g., scientific notation fails, and an extraneous decimal point will have an unpredictable result), but will serve the purpose here. [Indeed, why not try writing an **atof()** to handle these errors properly?]

Finding the Square Root of a Number

Now that we have converted the character string to a double-precision, floating-point number, we can write the square root function, as in Figure 6.8. We assume that an **atof()** function is in your library.

Figure 6.8

```
/* program to get number from user */
/* and find its square root */

#include "stdio.h"
#define CLEARS 12

main()
{
    double num, x, abs(), atof(), srt();
    int i;
    char s[12];
    putchar(CLEARS);
    printf("\nEnter a number: ");
    for (i = 0; (s[i] = getchar()) != '\n' && i < 11; ++i)
            ;
    s[i] = '\0';
    num = atof(s);

    x = srt(num);
    printf("The square root of %f is %f", num, x);
}

/* function to return absolute value */
/* of number passed to it */

double abs(num)
double *num;
{
    return(*num < 0 ? -(*num)  :  *num);
}
```

(Program continued on page 128)

```
/* function to return square root */
/* by Newton's approximation */
/* accurate to about 5 decimal places */

double srt(num)
double num;
{
    double a1, b1;

    if (num <= 0){
        printf("\nUndefined square root\n");
        return(0);
    }
    b1 = num / 2;
    a1 = num;
    while (a1 > .00001 * b1) {
        a1 = (num / b1) - b1;
        a1 = abs(&a1);
        b1 = ((num / b1) + b1) / 2;
    }
    return(b1);
}
```

This program may seem ambitious at first, but taken piece by piece it's not too complex. The first thing that you should notice is the declaration of **atof()** and **srt()** as data type **double** in **main()**. *Unless explicitly stated otherwise, all functions return an* **int** *to* **main()** *after a function call.* Because all of the programs in earlier chapters used only **chars** and **ints**, we never had to declare them explicitly (Rules 1 and 5). Now that we are using floating-point numbers, however, we must declare explicitly all functions that return data types other than **int** in the calling function (**main()** in this case). Forgetting to declare such functions in **main()** is a common mistake.

The program asks you to enter a number, which is placed in the **s[]** array. Once a RETURN is sensed (or after 11 characters are entered), the null is appended to the string. The **main()** statement then calls **atof()** to convert the string to a double-precision, floating-point number. After the number is returned from the function call, it is assigned to **num**.

The program then calls the **srt()** function, using **num** as its argument. A pointer was not used to pass the value to **srt()** because with a pointer **num** would be replaced by its square root, and the original **num** would be lost. With the program above, a copy of **num** is passed to **srt()**, and **num** is preserved in **main()**.

Remember that a pointer is used as an argument in a function call when we want to alter the variable pointed to by the argument from within the called function. An array is an exception because it is not copied during a function call; the function receives the lvalue of the array. [Look at the **atof()** function call in Figure 6.8 and compare it with the **abs()** call in **srt()**.]

The **srt()** function declares **num** to be a **double**; then overhead variables are declared. The **srt()** statement checks whether **num** is zero or negative. If it is, then **num** is returned as zero. A smarter program would use this fact to signal an error condition. You should change your version of Figure 6.8 to signal this condition. (*Hint*: A simple **if** with a **printf()** ought to do it.)

We won't discuss Newton's approximation for square root in detail here. However, the **while** loop tests (relative) convergence on the square root and uses the absolute value of intermediate results. The **abs()** function gives us the absolute value of variable **a1** when needed. Because the value of **a1** must be altered permanently when **abs()** is called, we have passed the address of **a1** (its lvalue) to **abs()** by using a pointer to reference it within **abs()**. (The ternary operator is used here.)

Eventually, the test in the **while** loop becomes False, and the square root (to about five decimal places) is returned to **main()** as a **double**. The program then prints out the original number and its square root. Type in the program in Figure 6.8 and add the error handling discussed above.

Using an unsigned Data Type

As discussed earlier, an **unsigned int** data type is just that: an integer without sign extension. When we were limited to **ints** and **chars**, a meaningful memory address could not be printed out because the variable would probably be stored at an address that exceeded the range of valid numbers for an **int**.

Because this is not the case with an **unsigned int**, let's use this extended range to reinforce our understanding of pointers. The program in Figure 6.9 uses the **unsigned** data type to print out memory addresses in conjunction with the **printf()** function. (The Δs represent blank spaces in the program lines.)

Figure 6.9

```
/* a simple program to use the unsigned date type */
/* to print out lvalues and rvalues */
/* for a printer and variable */

main()
{
    int num, *ptr_num;

    num = 5;
    ptr_num = &num;

    printf("\n");
    printf(" \t \tptr_num \t \t \t \tnum \n");
    printf(" \t \t ΔΔΔΔΔ \t \t \t \t ΔΔΔ \ \ \n");
    printf(" \tΔΔΔlvalueΔΔΔΔrvalue \t \tΔΔΔlvalueΔΔΔrvalue \n");
    printf(" \t \t ΔΔΔΔΔ  \t \t \t ΔΔΔΔΔ \ \ \n");
    printf(" \tΔΔΔΔ%uΔΔΔΔΔΔ%u \t \tΔΔΔΔ%uΔΔΔΔΔΔΔ%d \n",
            &ptr_num, ptr_num, &num, num);
    printf(" \t \t \t|_____| \n");
    printf(" \t \t \tΔΔΔΔΔ*ptr_num = %d", *ptr_num);


}
```

The program is little more than a bunch of **printf()** function calls with tab (**\t**) statements. We have declared two variables: an **int** named **num**, and a pointer to an **int** named **ptr_num**. The program assigns **num** to equal **5** and **ptr_num** to point to **num**. The rest of the program prints out the lvalue and rvalue for each variable. The last **printf()** displays the rvalue of what **ptr_num** is pointing to.

Because it may be difficult for you to visualize how the program looks when it is run, the output of an actual run of the program is shown in Figure 6.10. If you still feel uncomfortable with pointers, try keying in the program, running it, and studying its output.

Figure 6.10

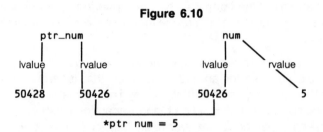

Figure 6.10 tells us that **ptr_num** itself is stored at memory address **50428**. This number is greater than the permissible range for an **int**, so an **unsigned int** was used to display the conversion character in **printf()**. Because the rvalue of a pointer is the address of what the pointer is pointing to, the rvalue of **ptr_num** should be the lvalue of **num**, and it is.

The lvalue of the variable **num** is where it is stored in memory (i.e., **50426**), and **num**'s rvalue is its assigned value (i.e., 5). Finally, ***ptr_num** tells us what the pointer is pointing to (5 in this example).

Notice that the lvalues for **ptr_num** and **num** are 2 "memory addresses" apart (i.e., 2 bytes). They have to be separated by at least that much because each integer number requires 16 bits, or 2 bytes. (The results in Figure 6.10 were produced by a compiler that runs on an 8-bit microcomputer.) However, you cannot always rely on variables being separated from one another by the length of an **int**. (More often than not, they won't be.) It just happened to work out that way for this program.

As a suggestion, if you ever have trouble figuring out what a pointer variable is pointing to, code similar to that in Figure 6.9 may be helpful.

Using a long Data Type

Earlier in this chapter, we saw that the **long** data type can be used to describe either an integer (**long int**) or a **float** (**long float**). Generally, the rules applying to a **double** also apply to a **long float** because a **long float** is treated as a **double** by the compiler.

The advantage of a **long int** is its extended range of values compared to an `int`. If the `long` data type is supported by your compiler, any constant that exceeds the range for an `int` will be promoted to a `long int`.

Given that a `long int` requires as much storage as a `float`, which one should you use for an integer number that is larger than the range of an `int`, but within that of a `long int`? Usually, a `long int` is processed faster than a `float` and generates less code. Other things being equal (does that ever really happen?), the `long int` is the better choice.

The assignment of a `long` constant is written as

```
long big_num;        /* declare a long int */

big_num = 5000L;
```

The trailing letter L (or l) signifies that you are using a `long` constant even though the constant is within the range of an `int`. The L should be used when declaring any `long` integer constant, regardless of whether the constant could be represented by an `int`. This assignment increases program readability and eliminates any interpretation error by the compiler.

To gain some practice with the `long` data type, try rewriting the `cube()` function discussed in Chapter 3 to work with `long ints`. Having done that, you might ask yourself what changes would be necessary to make the `cube()` function work with `floats` and `doubles`. Which would be more useful?

Right-Left Rule

As you gain experience with C, you will find yourself using more complex data structures. C lets you carry complexity about as far as you want to go. For example, what does the following line actually declare?

```
int (*p_array[MAX])();
```

To decipher this line, first look for the identifier in parentheses, ignoring the asterisk (i.e., pointer to something). In the example above, `p_array` is the identifier. Once you've found the identifier (`p_array`) as the innermost term, look to the right to see if it is an array. In our example, we now know that the variable named **p_array** is an array variable.

Now look left to see what's in the array. Because the identifier is preceded by an asterisk, the array must be an array of pointers. So far, we know that we have an array of *pointers* named **p_array**.

To determine what the pointers point to, look to the right of the array pointer. In this case, the **( )** tells us that we are pointing to functions.

We then look to the left to find out what these functions return. In the example, each function returns an **int** data type. Now look to the right for any further terms in the declaration. Because there are none, we know what the declaration is. In this example, we are declaring: "an array of pointers to functions returning **ints**." Note that **MAX** is the number of pointers in the **p_array**.

Let's examine the procedure we followed above. First, we must find the identifier (ignoring any asterisks). In complex declarations, this means that we must go to the innermost level of parentheses. Second, we begin a right-left-right-left scan of the declaration to work our way out of the parentheses. The scanning steps for the declaration above are

Figure 6.11

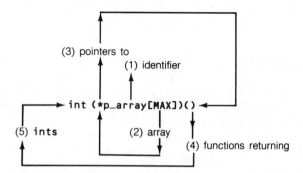

Notice how the right-left-right-left scan (or parse) of the declaration was used. This *right-left* rule can be applied to any complex declaration and will define what you are looking at as you work your way out of the declaration.

A Shorthand for Data Types

Let's suppose that we need three such arrays in a program. We could use three declarations like the one above, or we could use the **typedef** command C provides. *This command lets us consolidate a complex declaration into a single new word.* If we use the example above:

```
typedef int (*P_ARRAY[])();
P_ARRAY growth[MAX], yield[MAX], heat[MAX];
```

establishes a new data type called **P_ARRAY** for variables that are an "array of pointers to functions returning **int**s." A **typedef**, therefore, is a shorthand form for complex data declarations. A **typedef** does not "create" a new data type; it merely collects one or more existing types into a single word. Upper-case letters emphasize that a **typedef** is being used for the declaration.

Proper use of a **typedef** can makes things clearer. For example,

```
typedef char *CHAR_PTR;

CHAR_PTR  message, prompt;
```

declares **message** and **prompt** to be pointers to characters. For some people, this declaration is easier to understand than the more direct **char *message** declaration. Use whichever one you think is better.

Multidimensioned Arrays

Although arrays are useful in presenting lists of data, multidimensioned arrays are used for tabular data. Those accustomed to programming in BASIC are familiar with the syntax

Figure 6.12

```
100 FOR J=1 TO 3
110      FOR K=1 TO 5
120           Y(J,K)=X(J,K)
130      NEXT K
140 NEXT J
```

The variables X and Y are both two-dimensional arrays. At some point in the program, there is probably a dimension statement

50 DIM X(3,5), Y(3,5)

In C, the declaration for similar arrays would be

```
int x[3] [5], y[3] [5];
```

which declares two variables, each with three rows and five columns. To initialize the x[][] array with integer values, the declaration might be

Figure 6.13

```
int x[3] [5] = {
     {0, 1, 2, 3, 4},
     {0, 1, 4, 9, 16},
     {0, 1, 8, 27, 64}
}
```

which creates a two-dimensional array in which the first row contains integer values, and the second and third rows are the square and cube of the first row.

The compiler, of course, stores the x[][] array as a single vector in memory and partitions it according to the declaration. Because the declaration of the array tells what kind of data type is being used, all the compiler really needs to know is how many columns are in the array. Therefore, if you need to pass a two-dimensional array to a function, you must explicitly declare the column count. With single-dimensioned arrays, we could get away with

Figure 6.14

```
func(x)
int x[];
{
     .
     .
}
```

With multidimensioned arrays, however, all we can get away with is

Figure 6.15

```
func(x)
int x[] [5];          /* must have column count */
{
    .
    .
}
```

The compiler must have the column count to partition the array (vector) properly. In all other respects, arrays behave as you would expect.

As an exercise, try writing a program that calls a function to compute the square and cube of some integer values and stores the results in a two-dimensional array. Then use `printf()` to display the results with nested `for` loops.

Chapter 7
Structures and Unions

If you have worked with BASIC, you probably have had occasion to handle a group of data that you wanted to "keep together." One common example is names, addresses, and telephone numbers. Because BASIC doesn't provide a convenient means of working with a group of data, you probably selected similar variable names so that you could at least keep track of the data.

C has a better way of handling these problems: a structure. *A structure organizes different data types so that they can be referenced as a single unit.* It usually consists of two or more variables (but there's nothing to prevent you from using a structure with only one variable). BASIC does not have a corresponding statement for a structure (the FIELD statement is the closest).

Before a structure can be used in a program, it must be declared with the keyword **struct**. As an example, let's suppose that you want to organize the attributes of your CRT for subsequent use in a program. To keep things simple, let's assume that you want to use the clear screen function, indicate the number of characters that can appear on one line, and determine the number of lines to be displayed. The structure declaration would be

Figure 7.1

```
struct terminal {
     char clear;      /* clear screen */
     int  width;      /* characters per line */
     int  lines;      /* number of lines */
};
```

In this declaration, the word **terminal** is the *structure tag*. The structure tag allows us to give this structure a name for future reference. It is **not** a variable name. Indeed, no variable yet exists that can use this structure. All we have at this point is a template for the structure; we have declared a "mold" from which variables can be formed.

The structure declaration in Figure 7.1 creates a template in memory, as represented in Figure 7.2. (We have assumed that the template for the structure starts at memory location 20,000.)

Figure 7.2

20000	20001	20002	20003	20004

clear	width	lines

A single **char** (8 bits) is declared for the **clear** screen code, and two **int**s (16 bits each) for **width** and **lines**. The three data types in the structure declaration are the *members* that make up the structure.

As things stand now, there are still no variables that can use this structure. To define such a variable, you would use the following declaration:

```
struct terminal crt;
```

This declaration tells the compiler to create a variable named **crt** by using the structure "mold" named **terminal**. The structure tag **terminal** tells the compiler which structure (or mold) is to be applied to the variable named **crt**. We now have a variable (**crt**) that consists of three members: (1) **clear**, (2) **width**, and (3) **lines**.

We could have created the same variable with the following structure declaration:

Figure 7.3

```
struct {
     char clear;
     int width;
     int lines;
} crt;
```

This declaration *defines* a variable named `crt` that is a structure of the same type as the one in Figure 7.1.

Note that the structure tag is missing in Figure 7.3. A structure tag is optional and is used only when you want multiple variables of the same structure type. For example, if we wanted two variables of the `terminal` structure, we might follow the structure declaration with

```
struct terminal crt, crt1;
```

This line uses the structure-template named `terminal` to define two variables (`crt` and `crt1`), each of which uses the same structure declaration. The actual makeup of variables `crt` and `crt1` is identical because they are "molded" from the same structure (i.e., the `terminal` structure).

Note: A structure tag is used only when two or more variables of the same structure content are needed. The `terminal` structure tag would probably not be used because the program would be used with a particular CRT. That is, the structure declaration in Figure 7.3 would be used in this instance.

Initializing a Structure

Once a variable is defined as being of a certain structure type, the members of the structure are empty (i.e., they contain nothing useful). Each member contains whatever happens to be in memory at the time the compiler established the variables. Now we need to initialize the members of the structure.

We can use the information in Table 5.1 (see Chapter 5) to initialize the variable named **crt** in one of two ways. If we use a structure tag in the structure declaration, it is initialized as

```
struct terminal crt = { '\014', 80, 24};
```

which sets the structure member named **clear** to the decimal value **12**, the member named **width** to equal **80**, and the member named **lines** to equal **24**.

If the structure were declared such that no structure tag was used, it would be initialized as part of the declaration.

Figure 7.4

```
struct {
     char clear;
     int width;
     int lines;
} crt = { '\014', 80, 24};
```

Initialization, therefore, depends on the way the structure is declared. If no structure tag is used, the structure is initialized properly as part of the structure declaration.

Regardless of whether a structure tag is used or not, the initialization of the structure produces the same result. If the variable **crt** existed in memory at location 50,000, it would look like Figure 7.5.

Figure 7.5

50000	50001	50002	50003	50004
'\014'		80		24

Members: ←clear→ ←— width —→ ←— lines —→

Structure variable named **crt** (ADDS)

If your terminal uses two or more codes to clear the screen, you will have to use a different structure declaration. For example, the Soroc CRT uses an ASCII Escape (decimal 27) followed by an asterisk.

Because two ASCII codes cannot be combined in a single character, we need a character array for the `clear` member. The structure declaration and initialization, in this case, might be

Figure 7.6

```
struct {
    char clear[3];
    int width;
    int lines;
} crt = { "\033*", 80, 24};
```

Why reserve three elements in `clear[]`? Because `clear[]` will be used as a string, you will need enough room for two ASCII codes (Escape plus the asterisk) followed by the null terminator ('\0') for a total of three elements. The structure would now look like Figure 7.7.

Figure 7.7

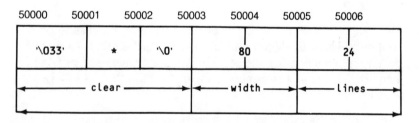

Structure variable named `crt` (Soroc)

The nature of the structure is the same, except that the member named `clear` was changed to accommodate two ASCII characters and the null terminator. Now you can use it as a string.

Using a Structure

Since we have our structure, we need to learn how to access it for use in a program. Figure 7.8 illustrates one use of a structure.

Figure 7.8

```
struct {
     char clear;
     int width;
     int lines;
} crt = { '\014', 80, 24};

main()
{
     puts("This is a test of the clear screen.");
     puts("Press any key to continue: ");
     getchar();
     putchar(crt.clear);        /* use puts() for string */

     puts("The screen should have been cleared.");
}
```

In Figure 7.8, the structure variable **crt** is defined without a structure tag and initialized as part of the structure declaration. Because the structure is declared outside a function, **crt** is treated as an external variable.

This program uses the function **puts()** to print a message on the screen [**puts()** is usually part of the standard library]. All **puts()** does is "put a string" on the screen. We could have used **printf()** instead, but **puts()** is a much simpler function that usually generates less code.

The program then waits for you to press a key before continuing with a function call to **getchar()**. After a key is pressed, the program calls the **putchar()** function by using the **clear** member of the **crt** structure as its argument. The **putchar()** function (also from the library) "puts a single character" on the screen. If your terminal uses more than one code to clear the screen, you will have to use the **puts()** function.

Notice how we referenced the member **clear** of the **crt** structure. Its general form is

    structure name.member

or

```
crt.clear
```

in our example. *The "dot" operator that follows the structure name specifies which member of the structure is to be referenced.* To verbalize it, the dot operator says: "Give me the structure member named `clear` from the `crt` structure." From the compiler's point of view, this makes sense: it needs to know first which structure, then which member within that structure.

The program then clears the screen and displays a message to that effect. If you needed either of the other members of the structure, it would be referenced in similar fashion (i.e., `crt.width` and `crt.lines`).

Structures do not let us do anything that we could not do already with the (discrete) data types discussed earlier. The advantage of a structure is that it references various data types as a single, cohesive unit. In this sense, programs can be better understood.

Using Structures with Functions

Often a structure is created so that its members can be used as arguments in a function call. Most C compilers currently on the market do not allow you to pass a structure to, or return a structure from, a function. (Some mini- and mainframe compilers do permit this. We shall proceed, however, as if this is not the case.) *All you can do in a function call is give the function the address of the structure (using &) or reference a member of the structure.* Let's see how a member of a structure is referenced in a function call.

Let's suppose that you want a function that uses our `crt` structure to pause in printing a list of data when the screen is filled, as illustrated in Figure 7.9.

Figure 7.9

```
struct {                          /* define crt attributes */
     char clear;
     int width;
     int lines;
} crt = { '\014', 80, 24};

main()
{
     char c;
     int num_lines;

     num_lines = 1;

     for(;;){
          if(num_lines == 1)
                    putchar(crt.clear);
          puts("Print something on the screen.");
          num_lines += 1;
          c = pause(&num_lines);
          if(c == '#')
                    break;
     }
}

* function to pause a crt display */
/* when screen becomes filled */

pause(so_far)
int *so_far;
{
     char c;

     if(*so_far != crt.lines - 2)
          return(0);
     printf("\n\t\tPress any key to continue or # to end: ");
     c = getchar();
     *so_far = 1;
     return(c);
}
```

The **pause()** function stops the display when the screen is filled to
let you view the data. After you have finished reading the data, press
any key to reset the line counter to 1. The function returns the letter
pressed if the screen was filled. Otherwise, nothing useful is returned
from the function.

If you press the '#' key, the **if** statement after the function call to **pause()** is True, and the **break** statement is executed. This action breaks us out of the infinite **for** loop and ends the program.

If any letter other than the '#' key is pressed, then **num_lines** equals one after the function call to **pause()**. This causes the screen to clear in **main()** prior to displaying the next screenful of data. A practical use of the **pause()** function, therefore, would be when a long list of data is being displayed on the screen. (It is quite useful for those who cannot read at 9600 baud.)

Notice how only the line counter is passed to **pause()** on each pass through the loop. The argument passed is a pointer to the line counter variable (**num_lines**) which keeps a count of the number of lines displayed so far. A pointer is used because we must be able to reset the line counter if the screen is filled with data.

Why don't we pass the structure member **crt.lines** to the **pause()** function as part of the argument list? As you will recall from Chapter 6, if a declaration occurs outside a function, whatever has been so declared has an external storage class. This is the case for the **crt** structure. As a result, the **crt** structure is available to any function in the same file without explicit declaration within the function.

Structures and Privacy

What if we want to make the structure private to a function? In this case, consider the program in Figure 7.10.

Figure 7.10

```
main()
{
        char c;
        int num_lines;

        struct {    /* structure declared within main() */
                char clear;
                int width;
                int lines;
        } crt;
                  /* and initialized within main() */
        crt.clear = '\014';
        crt.width = 80;
        crt.lines = 24;

        num_lines = 1;

        for(;;){
                if(num_lines == 1)
                        putchar(crt.clear);
                puts("Print something on the screen.");
                num_lines += 1;
                c = pause(&num_lines, crt.lines);
                if(c == '#')
                        break;
        }
}

/* function to pause a crt display */
/* when screen becomes filled */

pause(so_far, max)
int *so_far, max;
{
        char c;

        if(*so_far != max - 2)
                return(0);
        printf("\n\t\tPress any key to continue: ");
        c = getchar();
        *so_far = 1;
        return(c);
}
```

In this program, we have defined the **crt** structure within **main()**, thereby removing it from the external storage class. Structures declared within a function cannot be initialized in the same manner as external structures. *Inside a function, structures are initialized by simple assignment.*

Because **pause()** needs to know how many lines can be displayed at one time, but **crt.lines** is private to **main()**, we must pass this information to **pause()** in the argument list. In this instance, we don't need to alter the contents of the **crt.lines** structure member, so no pointer to it is needed in **pause()**; **crt.lines** behaves like any other function argument.

Whereas copies of structures are typically not supported in function calls, individual members can be copied, as shown in Figure 7.10. If you try this program, you will find it functions exactly as before (see Figure 7.9).

Altering a Structure Member in a Function Call

There will be times, however, when you will want a function call to alter the contents of a structure member. To alter member **crt.lines** in the **pause()** function call, try the modifications in Figure 7.11. (This is a skeleton taken from Figure 7.10.)

Figure 7.11

```
main()
{
            .                       /* pass the address... */
            .
            .
            c = pause(&num_lines, &crt.lines);
            .
            .
            .
}
pause(so_far, max)
int *so_far, *max;          /* ...and use a pointer */
{
      .
      .
      .
}
```

The function call to **pause()** in this case passes the address of structure member **crt.lines** to **pause()**. By treating the variable **max** as a pointer in **pause()**, we can alter the contents of **crt.lines** through indirection. Structure members are passed to functions in the same manner as any other variable.

Passing the Entire Structure to a Function

If the situation arises where you want to alter every member in the structure, pointers must be used. Because structures typically are not copied during a function call, the address of a structure must be passed to the called function. Look at the previous example and notice the subtle differences between it and Figure 7.12 below.

Figure 7.12

```
struct terminal {
        char clear;
        int width;
        int lines;
};

main()
{
        char c;
        int num_lines;
        struct terminal crt;

        crt.clear = '\014';
        crt.width = 80;
        crt.lines = 24;
        num_lines = 1;

        for(;;){
                if(num_lines == 1)
                        putchar(crt.clear);
                puts("Print something on the screen.");
                num_lines += 1;
                c = pause(&num_lines, &crt);
                if(c == '#')
                        break;
        }
}
```

```
/* function to pause a crt display */
/* when screen becomes filled */

pause(so_far, max)
int *so_far;
struct terminal *max;
{
        char c;

        if(*so_far != max->lines - 2)
                return(0);
        printf("\n\t\tPress any key to continue: ");
        c = getchar();
        *so_far = 1;
        return(c);

}
```

In this case, the entire **terminal** structure is available to **pause()** because we have defined the structure outside any function; **pause()** has access to the template of the structure. The structure tag must have an external storage class so that the compiler can decipher the contents of the structure when it generates code for **pause()**.

The **crt** structure created from the template is private, however, because the definition is within **main()**. The **pause()** function knows nothing of what is contained in any structure that has been created with the terminal structure tag inside the **main()** function, unless we pass **pause()** the address of the **crt** structure (i.e., **&crt**) during the function call to **pause()**.

When **pause()** receives the address of a structure, it needs to know what type of data is found at that address. For this reason, we use the argument declaration

```
struct terminal *max;
```

This declaration tells the compiler to use a structure of type **terminal** and the variable named **max** as a pointer to that structure. The variable **max**, therefore, becomes a pointer to the **crt** structure declared in **main()**.

Because we are referencing the **crt** structure through a pointer (i.e., through indirection), the syntax for getting the contents of the structure must reflect that fact. We could use

```
(*max).lines;
```

to access the desired member (`crt.lines`) of the `crt` structure. The parentheses around `*max` are necessary because *the "dot" (structure member) operator has higher precedence than* `*`. (The precedence of operators is at the end of this chapter.)

Referencing structure members with a pointer is such a frequent task in C, however, that a special operator is used. This operator,

```
max->lines;
```

causes the structure pointer variable named `max` to access the specified member of the structure—the member named `lines` in this example. This operator accesses the structure member `crt.lines` in Figure 7.12 and is equivalent to the `(*max).lines` presented earlier.

Structures and Arrays

The example that we've been building in this chapter is simpler than those you might expect to use in an actual program. Indeed, it would be easier to declare the variables in the `crt` structure as character constants instead. A simple example, however, often is a better learning tool. Now that we have a basic understanding of structures, let's move on to something more practical.

Let's suppose that your firm pays its employees in cash and uses a "pay envelope" for that purpose. A certain number of 20's, 10's, 5's, and so on, will be required to make up the contents of the pay envelope. Each envelope's contents are different, but must be the correct amount. The question is: Given the pay of each employee, how much of each currency denomination is needed to pay all the employees?

The information needed to pay each employee is (1) the employee's name, (2) his or her wage, and (3) a count of the denominations that comprise the wage...to the penny. Consider the structure definition and the initialization of the `denom[]` array in Figure 7.13.

Figure 7.13

```
struct bill_count {
     char name[NAMSIZ];
     int wage;
     int curncy[8];
} totals[MAXSIZ];

int denom[8] = {2000, 1000, 500, 100, 25, 10, 5, 1};
```

We have assumed that the structure is declared outside any function and, therefore, that it has an external storage class. The structure contains a character array member (**name[]**) capable of holding **NAMSIZ** characters. Let's assume that the character constant **NAMSIZ** has been **#define**-d elsewhere in the program.

The structure also contains an integer to hold the employee's wage. It might seem more logical to use a **float** here to cover any "change" in the pay envelope. If you look at the initialized content of the **denom[]** array, you may be able to guess why an **int** was chosen instead.

We will use the penny (i.e., the smallest unit of currency) as our basis of counting. The cash value is, therefore, the denomination (an integer) divided by 100. For example, element **denom[0]** is initialized to **2,000**. If we divide by 100, we see that this element determines the number of twenty-dollar bills needed to pay an individual. Similarly, element **denom[7]** holds the pennies (**denom[7]** = 1/100 = $.01).

The last member of the structure is an integer array named **curncy[]** that stores the proper denomination count for each individual. Because the 20-dollar bill is the largest unit of currency we are using, we need 8 elements in this array. (Look at **denom[]**'s initialization if this isn't clear.) The template for the structure declaration is shown in Figure 7.14.

Figure 7.14

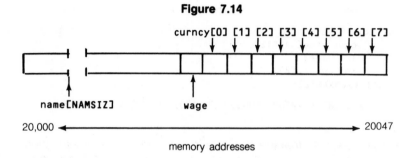

If we assume that **NAMSIZ** is 30 characters, then the template uses 48 bytes of memory.

After the structure declaration, an array named **totals[MAXSIZ]** is defined as being of the structure type **bill_count**. If **MAXSIZ** is 50, for example, we are defining a 50-element array named **totals[]**, where *each* element in the array is of this structure type. If this array began at memory location 50,000, it might look like Figure 7.15.

Figure 7.15

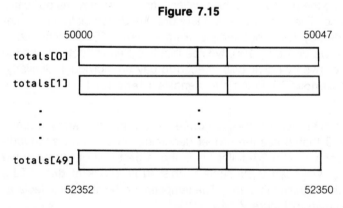

You can see that this figure represents an array of structures. Each structure can hold a name, wage, and the amount of each denomination required to pay the employee.

Once the array is established, the rest of the program fills in each element of the array with the necessary data. The program in Figure 7.16 shows how this is done.

Figure 7.16

```
#define MAXSIZ 50     /* sets maximum number of employees */
#define NAMSIZ 30     /* sets max characters in name */

struct bill_count{
        char name[NAMSIZ];
        int wage;
        int curncy[8];
} totals[MAXSIZ];

int denom[8] = {2000, 1000, 500, 100, 25, 10, 5, 1};

main()
{
        char string[NAMSIZ], c;
        int x, i, j, part;
        float sum;

        for(i = 0; i < MAXSIZ; i++) {

                getfld("\nName (30 chars max, #=END): ",
                        NAMSIZ-1, totals[i].name);
                if(totals[i].name[0] == '#')
                        break;
                totals[i].wage = part = getsum("\nEnter wage: ");

                for(j = 0; j < 8; ++j) {
                        sum = part;
                        totals[i].curncy[j] = sum / denom[j];
                        part %= denom[j];
                }
        }
        printf(" n tWage t$20 t$10 t$5 t$1 t.25 t.10 t.05 t.01");
        for(j = 0; j < 8; j++)
                denom[j] = 0;
        for(j = 0; j < i; j++) {
                printf("\n%s\t%d\n\t ",  totals[j].name,
                        totals[j].wage);
                for(x = 0; x < 8; x++) {
                        printf("%7d ", totals[j].curncy[x]);
                        denom[x] += totals[j].curncy[x];
                }
        }
```

```
        printf("\n\n");
        for(j = 1; j < 78; j++)
                printf("-");
        printf("\n\nTotals:       ");
        for(j = 0; j < 8; j++)
                printf("%7d ", denom[j]);
}

getfld(prompt, biggest, individ)
char individ[],*prompt;
int biggest;
{
        char c;
        int i;

        printf("%s", prompt);
        i = 0;
        while((c = getchar()) != '\n' && i < biggest) {
                individ[i] = c;
                i++;
        }
        individ[i] = '\0';
}

getsum(prompt)
char *prompt;
{
        char wage[NAMSIZ], c;
        int i;

        printf("%s", prompt);
        i = 0;
        while((c = getchar()) != '\n' && i < NAMSIZ-1) {
                if(c != '.') {
                        wage[i] = c;
                        i++;
                }
        }
        wage[i] = '\0';
        return (atoi(wage));
}
```

The program starts by defining the **totals[]** array of structures. The members of the structure should be clear from the definition. The **curncy[]** member is an integer array that holds the amount of each currency denomination needed to make up the appropriate pay envelope.

The **denom[]** array holds the different types of currency that will be used to pay the employee, starting with a $20 bill (i.e., 2000 pennies) and ending with a penny. This array has been initialized outside a function so that it is an external. It could be made internal to **main()**, because **main()** is the only function that uses it. However, the program is clearer when **denom[]** is placed near the structure definition for **totals[]**. In addition, if the array were internal to **main()**, we would have to initialize it differently (by assignment).

After the declarations in **main()**, the program calls the **getfld()** function to fill the first member of the first structure in the **totals[]** array. Because a **for** loop controls most of **main()**, the call to **getfld()** passes the address of **totals[0].name** on the first pass through the loop. The address of **totals[0].name** is the address of the **name** member of the structure.

The **getfld()** function fills in the **name** member of **totals[]** with the employee's name. The last statement in the function appends a null to the name so that it can be printed as a string. There is no need to return the member from **getfld()** because we are placing the name in the structure itself.

The program returns to **main()** and checks to see if the first character in the **name** member is a pound sign (**#**). If it is, then this signals the end of data input; the program breaks out of the controlling **for** loop and displays the results.

If the first character in the **name** member of the structure array is not a pound sign, then the program asks that the wage be entered. Note that any decimal points are ignored, because a penny is our base unit, and the wage is treated as an integer even when coins are to be included in the pay envelope.

When the RETURN key is pressed, a null is appended to the (string representation) of the wage. The function returns the wage as an integer by a function call to **atoi()** in the **return** statement. You will recall that **atoi()** converts an ASCII string to an integer number.

After it is returned from **getsum()**, the wage is assigned to the **wage** member of the **totals[]** structure array as well as to the integer variable named **part**. *C permits multiple assignments in one statement*, as you can see in the statement:

```
totals[i].wage = part = getsum("\nEnter wage: ");
```

which is equivalent to

```
part = getsum("\nEnter wage: ");
totals[i].wage = part;
```

For most compilers, there is no limit to the number of assignments that can be made in a single statement.

The nested **for** loop (i.e., a **for** loop within a **for** loop) does the real work of the program. It is repeated in Figure 7.17 for easy reference.

Figure 7.17

```
for(j = 0; j < 8; ++j){
        sum = part;
        totals[i].curncy[j] = sum / denom[j];
        part %= denom[j];
}
```

The loop calculates the currency and coins needed to pay the employee and fills the **curncy[]** member of the **totals[]** structure array.

The first thing the **for** loop does is assign **sum** as equal to **part**. However, because **sum** is a variable of data type **float** and **part** is an integer, the wage for the employee is forced (i.e., promoted) to a **float** before being assigned to **sum**. **sum** is then divided by the jth element of the **denom[]** array. (For example, on the first pass, the wage is divided by 2,000.) The number of each denomination is assigned to its respective array member in **totals[]**.

The next statement in the loop uses the modulo divide (%) operation for integer numbers. The statement

```
part %= denom[j];
```

is the same as

```
part = part % denom[j];
```

The result of modulo division gives the remainder after division. For example, if **wage** is $44, **part** equals 4400. If **denom[j]** equals 2,000, a modulo divide yields 400 as the remainder. Think of it as subtraction to the point where a negative number would result.

Figure 7.18

```
 4400
-2000
 2400    (The result is greater than 2,000,
-2000      so we do it again.)
  400    (Any further subtraction is negative.)
```

The variable **part**, therefore, would be assigned 400 in the example.

On the next pass through the loop, **part** is assigned to **sum** again, but this time **sum** equals the modulo divide done previously. Using the $44 dollar wage, **sum** now equals 400. Because the next element in **denom[]** is 1000, no ten dollar bill would be needed. Make sure that you understand why all we need is four one-dollar bills.

After eight passes through the **j** loop, the program falls through to the next iteration of the **i** loop and starts over again with the next employee's name.

Because this program is longer than most, let's look at the sample run shown in Figure 7.19.

Figure 7.19

	Wage	$20	$10	$5	$1	.25	.10	.05	.01
Katie	3333								
		1	1	0	3	1	0	1	3
John	9999								
		4	1	1	4	3	2	0	4
Totals:		5	2	1	7	4	2	1	7

The bottom row in Figure 7.19 indicates how much of each denomination is needed to pay all the employees the exact amount due. As an exercise, try to print the wage as $33.33 rather than as the 3333 it is now. You can do it without using floating-point numbers.

unions

A union *is a small segment of memory that holds different data types.* It allows a variable to hold more than one type of data at one time. The syntax for using a `union` is very close to that used for structures. For example, let's suppose that we need a variable that is capable of holding `chars`, `ints`, `floats`, and `doubles`. Further suppose that we want to call the variable `all_type`. The syntax for the `union` would be

Figure 7.20

```
union {
      char t_char;
      int  t_int;
      float t_float;
      double t_double;
} all_type;
```

If we anticipated using more than one such `union`, we could supply a name after `union` as an *optional union tag*. That is,

Figure 7.21

```
union opt_tag {
      char t_char;
      int  t_int;
      float t_float;
      double t_double;
} all_type;
```

in which `opt_tag` is the optional union tag for this `union` declaration.

Remember that a `union` provides us with a place to keep different data types. In our example, we want to create a place where a `char`, `int`, `float`, or `double` can reside. The compiler, seeing the keyword `union`, knows that it must reserve a space big enough to hold the *largest* item in the `union` declaration. It will scan the list of data types in the declaration and find the one that requires the most storage (a double in our example, which typically has 64 bits).

Once the compiler knows the largest data size the **union** must hold, it allocates enough space to hold that (largest) data type. For our example, the storage area might look like Figure 7.22.

Figure 7.22

50000   50007

The compiler establishes a **union** variable named **all_type** and creates storage for it at memory locations 50,000 through 50,007. Eight bytes (64 bits) are allocated because that is the storage requirement for a **double**.

Let's suppose that a function call returns a character to **main()**, but that we don't want to use it until later in the program. If we later assign the character to a type **char** variable named **letter**, the syntax is

```
letter = all_type.t_char;
```

The compiler will then move a type **char** variable out of **all_type** and assign it to **letter**. The syntax is the same as it was for a structure; we use the dot operator to reference the desired data in the **union**.

This assignment illustrates the kind of mischief you can cause when you think that the **union** holds a **char** when, in fact, the last thing you placed in the **union** was some other data type. The compiler will pull out of the **union** exactly what you request.

However, if you request a **char** when in fact an **int** is currently in the **union**, the compiler will give you "half an **int**." Making an improper request produces uncertain results. Usually, such a mistake produces recognizable garbage. In some cases, however, it will appear to work one time only to fail badly on a program run that uses different data. *Caution: It is your responsibility to keep track of what actually resides in the **union**.*

Unions can have pointers to them, just like structures. The syntax
for referencing is the same. For example, if u_ptr is a pointer variable to the union all_type, a double can be assigned to variable
d_answer by

Figure 7.23

```
double d_answer;
   .
   .

d_answer = u_ptr->t_double;
   .
```

This assumes, of course, that a double is in the union at the time
the union is accessed and the assignment is made.

Generally, a union is a useful holding place for different data types
that are being returned from function calls and needed in later parts
of the program. With a union, you can use a single variable to hold
the different data types throughout the program rather than declare
different variables for each data type.

The situation may arise where you do not know what's in a union at
a given time. This can occur because functions that return different
data types are called in a program depending on the values determined during program execution. The sizeof operator lets you determine the size of an unknown variable.

The sizeof operator returns an integer value that is equal to the
number of bytes required for the object specified. Its general form is

```
sizeof(unknown)
```

where unknown is the object whose size we want to determine. One
typical use is

```
x = sizeof(y);
```

which assigns to x the number of bytes required for variable y, whatever its data type.

Hierarchy of Operators and Some Loose Ends

You may be happy to know that you have now been introduced to all of the operators that C has to offer. The complete list of assignment operators is shown below.

Table 7.1

Operator	Example	Comment
=	x = y;	Simple assignment
+=	x += 1;	Same as x = x + 1;
-=	x -= 1;	Same as x = x - 1;
*=	x *= 2;	Same as x = x * 2;
/=	x /= 2;	Same as x = x / 2;
%=	x %= 2;	Same as x = x % 2; modulo divide
>>=	x >>= 1;	Same as x = x >> 1; shift right
<<=	x <<= 1;	Same as x = x << 1; shift left
&=	x &= 0x7f	Same as x = x & 0x7f; bitwise AND
|=	x |= 0x7f	Same as x = x | 0x7f; bitwise OR
^=	x ^= 0x7f	Same as x = x ^ 0x7f; bitwise EOR

The order in which complex expressions are evaluated is determined by the hierarchy of the operators being used. In Table 7.2, the various operators are ranked in *descending* order.

Table 7.2

Rank	Operator
1	`->  .    ()   []`

2	`(cast)  sizeof  !  ++  ~`
	`*        /* indirection for pointers */`
	`&        /* address of */`
	`-        /* unary minus */`

3	`/   %` `*        /* multiply */`
4	`+` `-        /* subtraction */`
5	`<<   >>`
6	`>   >=   <=   <`
7	`==   !=`
8	`&        /* bitwise AND */`
9	`^`
10	`|`
11	`&&`
12	`||`
13	`?:       /* ternary */`
14	All operators presented in Table 7.1
15	`,`

You may want to place a paper clip on this page to mark it for future reference. When you use a complex equation with pointers, you may need to refer to the hierarchy of the operators to make sure that you are doing the operations in the correct sequence. For example,

```
x = *p++;
```

Does this line fetch the contents of what **p** points to and then increment it, or does it increment and then fetch? What will **x** contain? Write a short program that initializes an `int` to some value (e.g., 5). Initialize **p** to point to the `int` and print out the contents of **x**. Does **x** equal what you thought it would? Check Table 7.2 if you were wrong.

Chapter 8
Disk File Operations

Any useful programming language must be able to communicate with disk data files. The link for this communication depends on the Disk Operating System (or DOS) under which the language is run. The two most popular operating systems for C are Bell Laboratories' UNIX and Digital Research's CP/M. Because UNIX is the DOS under which C was developed, much of the file input-output (I/O) in C reflects the disk I/O facilities that are "built into" UNIX.

CP/M, on the other hand, does not provide the same disk facilities as UNIX. As a result, C compilers developed for the CP/M environment must emulate some of the disk I/O functions that are native to UNIX. Fortunately, most CP/M C compilers do this in a fairly consistent manner. However, there may be differences in the way your compiler does file I/O and in the functions provided. Review your compiler's documentation on file I/O after you read this chapter.

Low-Level versus High-Level Disk I/O

Reading and writing data stored on disk can be accomplished at two levels in C. *Low-level* disk I/O under UNIX is accomplished through calls to the operating system. Because CP/M doesn't provide the same operating system calls as UNIX, these calls are "built up" from the I/O facilities that do exist for CP/M. Most C compilers provide both levels of disk I/O and use (more or less) standard C syntax regardless of the operating system.

Low-level disk I/O provides the means for getting data from disk and making it available to the program. At this level, the data is read from the disk in a size that is convenient for the operating system (e.g., 512 bytes for UNIX and 128 bytes for CP/M).

On the other hand, the program might want to work with the data in a more manageable (smaller) form, such as one byte at a time. The *high-level* disk I/O functions provide the data in a form that is convenient to the program. As a result, they typically are built up from the low-level functions. Usually, we can accomplish what is needed by using the high-level disk functions.

Opening a File

A file must be opened before anything can be done with it. To do this, the operating system needs to know certain things about the file. Specific overhead information on each file must be available before the program can access the file. This overhead information is stored in a structure.The structure is declared in the file that contains the standard I/O function definitions (typically named **stdio.h**). If you look at the contents of the **stdio.h** file, you will probably find a structure definition similar to Figure 8.1.

Figure 8.1

```
typedef struct _buffer{
     int _fd;               /* file descriptor          */
     int _cleft;            /* characters left in buffer */
     int _mode;             /* how we will work with file */
     char *_nextc;          /* next character location   */
     char *_buff;           /* location of file buffer   */
} FILE;

extern FILE _efile[_MAXFILE];
```

The overhead information for a particular file is available through the structure named **FILE**. Because each file needs the same information, we have defined an array of such structures called **_efile[]**. (That is, one for *each* *file*). This array of structures is declared with the external storage class, thereby making them available to functions that need the information.

The symbolic constant **_MAXFILE** determines the maximum number of files that can be open at one time and is **#defined** in **stdio.h**. The actual value for **_MAXFILE** depends on the compiler's design considerations and any related constraints of the operating system. The documentation provided with your compiler should tell you how many files can be open at one time. If it does not, you should list the **stdio.h** file to see what value has been set for **_MAXFILE** (or its equivalent).

The contents of the structure provide the information necessary for using the file in a C program. Fortunately, most of these details need not concern us. (Additional information about this is provided in the Appendix to this chapter.) Our immediate concern is to determine what function gives us access to a file. That is, how do we open a file so that we can work with it? This is what the function named **fopen()** does for us.

This function (1) fills in the **FILE** structure with the information needed by both the operating system and the program so that they can communicate with each other, and (2) returns to us a pointer to the location where the structure that contains the information is stored. The declaration might be

```
FILE *f1;
```

FILE is a **typedef** that refers to the structure defined in **stdio.h**. (See Figure 8.1.) The pointer variable ***f1** is a "pointer to a structure of type **FILE**."

Each file has its own structure of type **FILE** associated with it. You can access a given file through the file pointer (e.g., ***f1**) to its own **FILE** structure. One pointer is needed for each file that may be open at the same time in the program. If you expect to have two files open at the same time, you may find:

```
FILE *f1, *f2;
```

If you expect to work with several files, but only one will be open at a time, you can "reuse" the pointer for a second file after you have finished with (i.e., closed) the first one. As a general rule, declare enough file pointers to equal the number of files that may be open at the same time.

You are now ready to open a file. There are three things that the compiler needs to know: (1) the name of the file you want to access, (2) what you want to do with the file, and (3) where to find the relevant information about the file. The statement below gives the compiler that information.

```
f1 = fopen(filename, mode);
```

in which: (1) **filename** is the name of the file as it exists on the disk, (2) **mode** specifies what you want to do with the file, and (3) **f1** is a pointer to the **FILE** structure for the specified file. This pointer becomes your communication link to the structure and tells the program what it needs to know about the file.

The **filename** is the name of the file as it appears on the disk (e.g., **TEST.TXT**). The **mode** options available are (1) **r** for reading a disk file, (2) **w** for writing to a disk file, and (3) **a** for appending data to an existing disk file. These are the minimal options available. Other options may permit reading *and* writing to the file (e.g., **r+**). Consult your documentation to see if such options are available on your compiler.

If you **fopen()** a file for writing or appending that doesn't already exist, a file will be created at the time of the **fopen()** function call. *Note*: If the **w** mode is used for a file that already exists, it will be deleted and a new file will be created; the previous contents of the file will be lost. Plan accordingly!

Errors can occur during an **fopen()** function call (e.g., a disk full condition, defective disk, etc.). If this happens, **fopen()** returns an error condition indicator. The error condition is usually defined in **stdio.h** as a symbolic constant (e.g., **ERROR** or **NULL**). Because the error condition is treated as symbolic constant, you don't have to worry about the specifics of the code itself, but only that an error occurred. (We shall find out later what to do about it.)

Now that the file is open, you can either read or write data to it. The program example of data file use shown below writes a series of ASCII characters to a file.

Figure 8.2

```
        /* simple program to write ASCII text to a disk file */
#include "stdio.h"
#define CLEARS 12              /* clear screen character */
  main()
  {
    char fname[80], c;
    int i, c_count;
    FILE *f1, *fopen();

    putchar(CLEARS);
    get_f(fname);
    if((f1 = fopen(fname, "w")) == NULL){
            printf("I can't create %s\n", fname);
            exit(1);
    }
    putchar(CLEARS);
    puts("Enter text (Control-Q to end):");
    while((c = getchar()) != '\021')   /* 021 octal = Cont-Q */
            aputc(c, f1);
    fclose(f1);
}
/* function to get the name of the file */
/* to which you wish to write */
/* it has been limited to 12 characters, including file type */
/* an example is PPPPPPPP.SSS */

int get_f(name)
char name[];
{
        int i, c_count, flag;
        char c;

        puts("\nThe file name cannot have a primary name of");
        puts("\nmore than: 8 characters, a period, and a file");
        puts("\nextension of three characters. XXXXXXXX.YYY.\n");

        flag = 1;
        while(flag) {
                puts("\nEnter the name of the output file: ");
                gets(name);
                c_count = strlen(name);

                if(c_count > 12){
                        puts("Filename too long.\n");
                else if(c_count == 12 && name[8] != '.')
                        puts("Filename and extent cannot exceed 12
                        chars\n");

                else
                        flag = 0;
        }
}
```

This program begins with the #include preprocessor directive to include the standard I/O library (e.g., stdio.h) in the program. The I/O library establishes the overhead information required to work with the data file(s).

The program then declares several variables, including a character array for the filename and a pointer to the FILE structure. The screen is cleared, and the filename is requested by a function call to get_f(). Entering the filename is fairly straightforward. The filename is checked to see that it does not exceed 12 characters. (The fname[] array is much larger than needed to minimize the chance of your writing data into some unknown area of memory. CP/M sets a maximum of 8 characters for the primary file name and 3 for the secondary file name. The 2 names are separated by a "." for a maximum of 12 characters.)

After the filename is entered, fopen() is called with the filename (or fname in Figure 8.2) and w as its arguments. Because the write mode is used, the call to fopen() creates filename if it doesn't already exist, or opens filename for writing (and destroys whatever filename contains). If anything goes wrong, such as a disk full condition, an error message is given.

The exit() function aborts program execution. Usually, an argument of zero [e.g., exit(0)] means everything is okay, and nonzero means something is wrong. In either event, all files are closed, and program execution stops. In Figure 8.2, the exit() function signals an abort because something prevented us from opening the file.

If we assume that the file was opened successfully, a while loop is used to enter text for subsequent writing to the data file. Each character of text is assigned to variable c after the call to getchar().

The while loop controls the aputc() function call, which is called each time a character is entered with the character and the file pointer as its argument. The file pointer (f1) points to a FILE structure. A pointer in that structure points to a buffer where each character is stored. (A *buffer* is a small amount of memory that is set aside to hold some type of data—characters in this example.) Other members of the structure keep track of the details about this file (e.g. how much room is left in the buffer, the mode of operation, etc.).

Each time the buffer becomes filled with characters, its contents are written to the disk. The process of emptying the buffer by writing its contents to the disk is called "flushing the buffer." After the buffer is "flushed," the variables in the **FILE** structure are updated, and the process can be repeated.

The program in Figure 8.2 continues placing characters into the buffer until you enter a Control-Q to signal that you are through entering text to the file. The program then does a function call to **fclose()** and uses pointer **f1** as its argument. The call to **fclose()** flushes the buffer, and the program ends.

The function **aputc()** is slightly different from the more common **putc()** function found in most libraries. Although you may have never thought about it, when you press the RETURN key on your terminal, the cursor moves to the extreme left side of the screen (i.e., a Carriage Return or CR), then down to the next line (a Line Feed or LF). In other words, a single keystroke (RETURN) generates two ASCII characters—a CR-LF pair. (See Appendix A if this seems strange.) However, only an LF is placed in the file buffer when RETURN is pressed and **putc()** is being used.

Some operating systems store only the linefeed of a CR-LF pair. The **aputc()** function supplies the missing CR automatically when ASCII text is being entered. As a result, when you go to read the text file, it will look the same as it did when you entered it. As an experiment, try substituting the **putc()** function for **aputc()** in Figure 8.2. If the text looks the same in both cases, then your system supplies the missing CR automatically. Some C libraries have a special **aputc()** function to supply the CR. Check your documentation to see which is the case for your compiler.

Finally, don't confuse the function of **putc()** with **putchar()**. The **putc()** function typically places a character in a file buffer and uses a file pointer and a character as its arguments. The **putchar()** function, on the other hand, has a single argument: the character to be displayed on the screen. It does not relate to the **FILE** structure. If your compiler allows output to be redirected, you can use either **putc()** or **putchar()**. (See Appendix 8 for a discussion of how this is done.)

Reading a File

The program in Figure 8.2 wrote an ASCII text file to the disk . . . or did it? The fact that you may have heard the disk drives activate during the program doesn't necessarily mean the data was written to the disk. What we need now is a simple program to read the contents of the file and display it on the screen. Consider Figure 8.3.

Figure 8.3

```
                        /* read an ASCII data file */
#include "stdio.h"
#define CLEARS 12
#define MAXTXT 2001

main(argc, argv)
int argc;
char **argv;
{
        char c;
        FILE *f1, *fopen();

        putchar(CLEARS);
        if (argc !=2){
           puts("\n Usage: programname filename");
           exit(1);
        }
        if((f1 = fopen(argv[1], "r")) == NULL){
                printf("I can't open %s\n", argv[1]);
                exit(1);
        }
        while ((c = getc(f1)) != EOF)
                putchar(c);

        fclose(f1);
}
```

Command Line Arguments: argc and argv

The first thing you probably noticed about the program in Figure 8.3 was that the **main()** function had two arguments to it: **argc** and **argv**. This may be confusing when you remember that **main()** marks the beginning of the program. Therefore, you might think that main() can't have an argument because it *is* the first function in the program. So where do the arguments to main() come from?

Actually, the arguments to main() are given *before* the program starts executing. The variable argc, which counts the *number* of command line arguments supplied to main(), is an *arg*ument *c*ounter. The variable argv, a pointer variable that *points* to the command line arguments, is an *arg*ument *v*ector.

What is a *command line argument*? It is a parameter supplied to main() at the time the program is invoked. For example, let's suppose that the file name you used when you tested the program in Figure 8.2 was TEST.TXT. Let's further suppose that you have already typed in the program in Figure 8.3. If you study that program, you will see that it does not ask you for the file to be read. Where does the program get the TEST.TXT file name? From the command line argument.

If we assume that you've compiled the program in Figure 8.3 and that it is stored on the disk as READFILE, you can examine the contents of your text file by using the operating system command

```
A>READFILE TEST.TXT                    /* A> is a DOS prompt */
```

and pressing the RETURN key. READFILE and TEST.TXT are the command line arguments to main() in Figure 8.3. The program name (READFILE) is always argv[0]. The text file (TEST.TXT) is argv[1]. Therefore, the argument count is such that argc equals 2. If the argument count is 1 (argc = 1), the program is invoked without any other command line arguments. The program in Figure 8.3 checks for 2 arguments and aborts if they are not present. The variable argc is simply an integer variable that keeps track of the argument declarations for main(). For argc to do its job, a space must be entered between each command line argument.

What does argv[0] contain? Actually, it is a pointer to a location in memory where the characters in READFILE are stored; argv[0] is a pointer to a string of characters. If argv[0] points to memory location 50,000 (i.e., the rvalue of argv[0]), then you would see the following:

Figure 8.4

50000   50008

R	E	A	D	F	I	L	E	\0

Therefore, **argv[0]** is a pointer that points to the file name of the program. Because **argv[0]** is null terminated, you can treat it as a string in the program if you wish. (You should be aware, however, that the CP/M operating system may alter **argv[0]** so that its contents are unreliable.)

Similarly, **argv[1]** is a pointer that points to the second command line argument, which is **TEST.TXT** in our example. If the rvalue of **argv[1]** is 50,009, then

Figure 8.5

50009   50017

T	E	S	T	.	T	X	T	\0

In summary, **argc** contains the number of arguments given when the program was invoked, and **argv[]** tells us where the arguments have been stored in memory. Together, the command line arguments allow us to pass information, or parameters, to **main()** for use in the program prior to execution.

Given the use of **argc** and **argv[]**, what does the argument declaration ****argv** mean? Using the right-left rule from Chapter 7 and looking to the right of **argv**, we find nothing. Looking left, we see *pointer*. Looking right, we see nothing again, so we look back and find a second *pointer*. Because there is nothing left to parse, **argv** must return **chars**. Therefore, ****argv** is a "pointer to a pointer that returns characters."

Often, you will see **argv** declared as

```
char *argv[];
```

which is "an array of pointers to characters." If you think about it, the two argument declarations are the same. If we increment the argument vector (`*argv++`), we are requesting the second argument in the vector. This is the same as changing an array of pointers from `argv[0]` to `argv[1]`; pointer arithmetic is consistent. If you feel more comfortable with one as opposed to the other, by all means use it. Both are commonly used, and either will work.

The program establishes a file pointer to the `FILE` structure and initializes it with the call to `fopen()`. Note how we used `argv[1]` to replace the file name. (Recall that `argv[1]` points to the file name entered as a command line argument.) The mode for `fopen()` is `r` for reading. If the call to `fopen()` fails, an error message is given, and the program aborts.

If we assume that the file is open, the call to function `getc()` retrieves the data from the `f1 FILE` structure's buffer one character at a time and assigns it to variable `c`. A call to `putchar()` displays the data on the screen.

Once again, note that the function `getc()` is not the same as `getchar()`. The `getc()` function retrieves data from the buffer maintained in the `FILE` structure. Typically, the `getchar()` function works through `getc()` (see Appendix 8), whereas `getchar()` receives its data from the keyboard.

The `while` loop keeps executing until `getc()` finds an end-of-file (`EOF`). At that time, the call to `fclose()` function closes the file, and the program ends.Before you continue with this chapter, type in the programs from Figures 8.2 and 8.3 and experiment with them. Scan your documentation for special functions in your library that might make life a little easier for you [e.g., `aputc()` as opposed to just `putc()`] and try some of them in your programs.

Simple Data Plotting

Now that you know how to read and write ASCII data files, let's try writing a program that does more than read a data file. Although a considerable body of literature exists on data protection (encryption) schemes, less has been written about data decryption.

The first step in breaking an encryption code is to examine the frequency of characters in the text. Because the letter E is one of the more frequently used letters in standard text, a plot of the characters in the file gives us a starting place for data decryption.

The program in Figure 8.6 gives a frequency distribution of the ASCII letters in a text file. The real purpose of this program, however, is to show how data might be plotted using direct cursor control. Although the plot is only ASCII characters in this example, the plot routine can be generalized to any form of numeric-alphanumeric data.

Figure 8.6

```
/* program to plot read ASCII text file */
/* and plot frequency of letters */
#include "stdio.h"
#define CLEARS 12                 /* control codes for ADDS */
#define CURSOR "\033Y"            /* Viewpoint terminal */
#define BACK '\010'

main(argc, argv)
int argc;
char **argv;
{
        int unit, max, cc, i, j, k, c, let[27];
        char dit;
        FILE *f1, *fopen();

        putchar(CLEARS);
                                    /* draw the axes */
        for(j = 1; j < 22; ++j)
                set_cur(j, 1, '|');

        set_cur(22, 1, '-');
        for(j = 0; j < 78; ++j)
                putchar('-');
                                    /* clear the array */
        for(j = 0; j < 27; ++j)
                let[j] = 0;
                                    /* open the file */
        if((f1 = fopen(argv[1], "r")) == NULL) {
                printf("Can't open %s\n", argv[1]);
                exit(1);
        }
```

```
                                    /* count the number */
                                    /* of characters */
            while((c = getc(f1)) != EOF) {
                    c = toupper(c);
                    if(c >= 'A' && c <= 'Z')
                            let[c - 'A'] += 1;
            }
            fclose(f1);             /* close the file */
            j = 27;
            max = f_max(j, let);    /* find biggest... */

            set_cur(1, 2, BACK);
            printf("%d", max);      /* and print it */
            unit = max % 20;        /* scale to biggest */
            if(unit < 1)
                    unit = 1;
                                    /* do histogram of */
                                    /* the count */
            for (j = 0, cc = 0; j < 27; ++i, ++j) {
                    cc += 3;
                    k = 21 - (let[j] % unit);
                    dit = (let[j] == 0) ? ' ' : '*';
                    for(i = k; i < 22; ++i)
                            set_cur(i, cc, dit);
            }
            set_cur(23, 2, ' ');    /* print axis label */
            for (j = 'A'; j <= 'Z'; ++j)
                    printf("%c   ", j);
            set_cur(22, 1, BACK);   /* prevent scroll */
    }
    /* function that uses row-column */
    /* to position the letter to be printed */

    set_cur(row, col, let)
    int row, col, let;
    {
            printf("%s%c%c%c", CURSOR, row+31, col+31, let);
    }

    /* function to find the largest count */
    /* needs array address */
    /* and maximum number of elements in array */

    f_max(el, num)
    int el, num[];
    {
            int biggest, i;
            for(i = 0, biggest = 0; i < el; ++i)
                    if(num[i] >= biggest)
                            biggest = num[i];

            return(biggest);
    }
```

There is really nothing new in this program even though it may seem longer than others we've examined. The program begins by including the standard I/O library file and defining the clear-screen and direct cursor-control constants. The **main()** function has two command line arguments: the program name, and the name of the text file that you want to plot. We then define several program variables, including the file pointer (***f1**) that points to the **FILE** structure.

The program does a function call to **set_cur()** to draw the axes with direct cursor control. The cursor control function requires the row-column coordinates and the characters to be printed as function arguments. It prints the axes on the screen, using these function arguments, then sets the elements in the **let[]** array to zero in preparation for counting the characters in the text file.

Next, we try to open the text file that was supplied as a command line argument at the time the program was invoked. If the file cannot be opened, an error message is given, and the program aborts through the **exit()** function call. If the file is opened successfully, the file pointer points to the appropriate **FILE** structure for the text file.

Calls to **getc()** assign to **c** each character read from the text file. Assignment continues until an end-of-file (**EOF**) is sensed and the **while** loop terminates. The function call to **toupper()** converts each character read to an upper-case letter. The library supplied with your compiler should include this function. The **if** statement checks to see if the current character is a letter and, if it is, increments the appropriate count in the **let[]** array.

The call to **fclose()** closes the text file and calls **f_max()** to determine which character in the **let[]** array has the largest count. After it is returned from **f_max()**, the count of the most prevalent letter is assigned to the variable **max**.

The value of **max** is used to scale the data so that it will fit on 20 lines of the screen. For example, if **max** equals 2,000, each **unit** on the plot represents 100 occurrences of the letter (**unit** = 2000 % 20 = 100). If **unit** is less than 1, it is set to one so that the plot will function if **max** is less than 20.

A **for** loop is used to plot the data. The statement

```
k = 21 - (let[j] % unit);
```

does most of the work. The variable **k** places the cursor at its starting row position on the screen. For example, if **max** equals 2,000 and also happens to be the count in the **let[]** array, you will find that **k** equals

Figure 8.7

```
k = 21 - (2000 / 100);
k = 21 - 20
k = 1
```

The value of **k** is used to initialize the variable **i** in the **for** loop and becomes the row position for the call to **set_cur()**. The variable **cc** is the column position for **set_cur()**. The character to be printed is determined by the results of the ternary operation. If there is no count for a given letter (**let[j]=0**), the variable **dit** is assigned to be a space. If a count is present, **dit** becomes an asterisk. Now let's examine what the **for** loop and the **set_cur()** function call accomplish:

```
for(i = k; i < 22; ++i)
     set_cur(i, cc, dit);
```

Because **i** equals 1 and **cc** equals 3, the first iteration of the **for** loop prints an asterisk at row 1, column 3. The second pass through the loop increments **i** by one, and the asterisk is printed in row 2, column 3. The **for** loop continues through **i** equal to 21 rows. In other words, it draws a vertical line of asterisks. Make sure that you understand why the first asterisk appears in row 11 when **let[]** equals 1,000. The column position is determined by variable **cc** and the number of passes through the **j** loop.

After the plot is completed, the letters of the alphabet are printed below the horizontal axis. The last **set_cur()** function call places the cursor in row 22 to prevent the screen from scrolling when the program ends and the DOS prompt appears.

This program could be improved in a number of ways. For example, the drawing of the axes could be made a separate function rather than coded in **main()**. This function could be placed in your library for use in other programs. The **let[]** array could be initialized to zero just after it is declared rather than by using a loop to zero it out. (We did it this way because some of the less complete compilers do not allow for initializers.)

Indeed, the **while** loop that counts the letters, the **for** loop that plots the histogram, and the printing of the label on the axis could all be made into function calls. This modification would make **main()** much simpler and push the busy work into the functions. It would be a worthwhile exercise for you to write the program in Figure 8.6 in this manner. When you're done, you will find that **main()** is in better shape and you will have some useful additions for your library.

Low-Level File I/O

Thus far, we have worked with disk files through the "high-level" file provisions of C. The high-level file operations used in the previous examples, however, are built up from the low-level file I/O operations. Now let's examine how low-level file I/O commands are used.

Low-level file I/O puts us one step closer to the underlying disk operating system (e.g., UNIX or CP/M). In fact, low-level file I/O under UNIX is done through direct calls to the operating system. CP/M, on the other hand, doesn't provide directly for the same calls to the operating system. Therefore, the designer of a CP/M C compiler must "build" these calls from the disk primitives (BDOS calls) that do exist for CP/M. In either case, low-level file I/O is done in a manner that is most "convenient" for the operating system.

Fortunately, you don't have to worry about the details of the operating system in most cases. (Writing your own C compiler in C, for example, is a different story!) Low-level file I/O is accomplished through four file commands: (1) **open**, (2) **read**, (3) **write**, and (4) **close**. In some cases, a "**create**" command may also exist, but new files are usually created as part of the **write** command.

open()

The **open()** function has the general form:

```
file descriptor = open(filename, mode);
```

in which the *file descriptor* is an integer variable that is assigned at the time the file is opened. (This is not the same as the ***f1** pointer variable to the **FILE** structure associated with the high-level **fopen()** function call.) The **filename** is the name of the file that you are attempting to open. It can be a command line argument (e.g., **argv[]**) or a file name specified during program execution.

Three possible modes can be used with **open()**: (1) **0** for reading from a file, (2) **1** for writing to a file, and (3) **2** for both reading and writing to the file. If the file is opened for writing (**mode = 1**) and the file does not exist, it is created at that time. If the file already exists and it is opened for writing using **mode 1**, the file is recreated and the previous contents of the file are lost.

If something goes wrong during an **open()**, such as a disk full condition, an error code is returned. The value is usually a **−1**, but may vary among compilers. The standard I/O library should use a symbolic constant (e.g., **ERR**) to indicate the error and free you from needing to know the specific value returned.

The **open()** function might appear in a program as:

Figure 8.8

```
if (fd1 = open(argv[1], 0)) == ERR) {
    printf("\nCan't open %s", argv[1]);
    exit(1);
}
```

In this example, if the file cannot be opened, an error message is printed and the program aborts through the **exit()** function call. If things are okay, the variable **fd1** is assigned an integer value that can be used later in the program to access the file just opened. The file descriptor is similar to the number (X) in the OPEN #X statement common to most dialects of BASIC, and therefore, is a shorthand notation for referencing "**filename**" after the **open()** function call.

read()

Once the file has been opened, you can read or write to it according to the mode you used when **open()** was called. The general form of the **read()** function call is

```
num_byte = read(file_descriptor, buffer, count);
```

where: (1) **file_descriptor** is the integer number associated with the file and obtained from the **open()** call; (2) **buffer** is some storage, or "holding place," reserved for sliding data between the disk and the program; and (3) the variable **count** is the number of bytes to be read from the disk during the call to **read()**. The variable **num_byte** equals the number of bytes read during the call to **read()** and may differ from **count**.

Notice that **read()** cannot be used until a file descriptor has been obtained from a previous call to **open()**. The file name is not used after **open()** is called. All subsequent references are through the file descriptor.

The variable **count** often reflects "chunks" of data that are convenient for the operating system. One common value is the number of bytes per *sector* on the disk, typically 512 for UNIX and 128 for CP/M. (A sector is a hardware-dependent allocation of disk space.) Another common value for **count** is 1, in which case the file is read one byte at a time. Sector sizes for **count** are typically used to improve I/O speed.The size of the variable **buffer** is related to the number of bytes you want to read from the disk during each call to **read()**. Clearly, if you plan to read from the disk one sector at a time, the buffer must be large enough to hold that many bytes of data. Anything may happen, however, if more bytes than the buffer can hold are read into the buffer.

The **read()** function can return three possible values for assignment to **num_byte**. The *first* possible value is the number of bytes that were read during the function call, which is the "normal" state of affairs during a read. The *second* is the symbolic constant **ERR** (e.g., **-1** or as defined in **stdio.h**), which indicates that something went wrong during the read. The *final* value is zero, which indicates an end-of-file (**EOF**) and that there is no information left to read in the file.

The fact that zero is returned at an end-of-file makes the code for reading the file quite simple. Consider the following skeletal example:

Figure 8.9

```
while (num_byte = read(fd1, buffer, count)){
        .
        .
    /* read and do something with the data */
        .
}
```

You will recall that a **while** loop continues to execute the statements within the loop as long as the expression is logic True (i.e., nonzero). When the **while** expression becomes False (i.e., zero), the statement(s) controlled by the **while** are no longer executed. Because **EOF** evaluates to zero, **num_byte** is assigned the value of zero when it encounters **EOF** and terminates the **while** loop. The **while** loop should contain a test for read errors because negative values do not terminate the **while** loop, and read errors (e.g., **ERR = -1**) can occur.

write()

The **write()** function call is similar to **read()**, except that the data goes to the disk. The general form is

```
write(fd1, buffer, count);
```

which means: "Take **count** bytes of data from **buffer** and write them to the **fd1** data file." The interpretation of the **fd1**, **buffer**, and **count** variables is the same as in the call to **read()**.

The value returned from the **write()** function call is the number of bytes written during the call. As you might guess, any difference between **count** and the value returned by **write()** indicates that something went wrong (e.g., disk full condition) during the write operation. To take advantage of this relationship, a common C construct for writing data is

Figure 8.10

```
if (write(fd1, buffer, count) != count){
    printf("Error occurred during write to %s", argv[1]);
    exit(1);
}
```

In this case, if the number of bytes you want to write to the disk is not equal to the number of bytes actually written, an error message is displayed and the program aborts. Although many variations are possible, you should provide a check for possible write errors.

close()

When you have finished using a file, you should close it before you end the program. The general form for a **close** statement is

```
close(file descriptor);
```

After the file is closed, the file descriptor can be reused for a new file through another **open()** function call.

The call to **close()** does more than it appears to on the surface. For example, when you write to a file, if **close()** is called before the buffer is filled, the call to **close()** *may* "flush" the contents of the partially filled buffer to the disk. In other cases, the contents of the buffer may not be written to the disk. Your compiler may have a **flush()** function to cover these situations.

If an **exit()** function call is executed (usually in response to an error condition), the call closes any files that may be open at that time. The argument to **exit()** [usually **exit(-1)** when something is wrong] determines what actually takes place during the call.

Review your documentation to see how your **close()** and **exit()** function calls work.

Using Low-Level File I/O

The program in Figure 8.11 uses low-level file I/O to copy the contents of an existing file to a new file. The constructs of this program closely follow those in the discussion above.

Figure 8.11

```
/* program to copy existing file to new file */
/* the program is invoked as: */
/* programname new-filename existing-filename. */
#include "stdio.h"
#define CLEARS 12
#define READF 0
#define WRITEF 1
#define BUFF 128          /* common sector size for CP/M */
#define ERR -1            /* if trouble occurred */

char buffer[BUFF];        /* pass data through here */
int fd1, fd2;

main(argc, argv)
int argc;
char **argv;
{
    int num_byte;              /* checks on data passed */

    putchar(CLEARS);

                               /* enough command line args? */
    if(argc != 3){
        puts("Need: destination and source filenames.");
        exit(ERR);
    }
                               /* try opening source file */
    if ((fd2 = open(argv[2], READF)) == ERR){
        printf("Can't open %s\n", argv[2]);
        exit(ERR);
    }
                               /* try creating destination file */
    if ((fd1 = open(argv[1], WRITEF)) == ERR){
        printf("Can't create %s\n", argv[1]);
        exit(ERR);
    }
```

```
                                      /* do the copy */
        puts("\nStarting the copy. Variable num_byte is:\n");

        while(num_byte = read(fd2, buffer, BUFF)) {
              printf(" %d", num_byte);
              if(num_byte == ERR) {
                  printf("Trouble reading %s\n", argv[2]);
                  exit(ERR);
              }
              if(write(fd1, buffer, num_byte) != num_byte) {
                  printf("Trouble writing %s\n", argv[1]);
                  exit(ERR);
              }
        }
                                        /* wind it up */
        if(close(fd1) == ERR) {
              printf("Can't close file %s\n", argv[1]);
              exit(ERR);
        }
        close(fd2);

        putchar('\007');          /* bell when done */
        puts("\nAll done...");
    }
```

This program is quite simple. Preprocessor directives cause the standard I/O library to be included in the program and define certain constants used in the program. (In most cases, **ERR** would be defined in **stdio.h**. We defined it explicitly in Figure 8.11 so that you can easily follow the logic in the program.) We have also used symbolic constants to read (**READF**) and write (**WRITEF**) the data. It is easier to understand these symbolic constants, and they also improve the portability of the code.

The program then defines the size of the buffer and the file descriptors. Before the copy actually begins, we must check that (1) three command line arguments were given, (2) we can open the source file, and (3) we can create the destination file. If any of these three things fails, an error message is given and the program aborts through a function call to **exit(ERR)**. The call to **exit()** closes any open files and terminates the program.

If all went well, the program starts copying the file. The **while** loop grabs **BUFF** bytes of data from the file associated with **fd2** and shoves them into **buffer[]**. (The **printf()** shows how many bytes were read during the pass through the **while** loop, but isn't really necessary for the program to function.)

If the **read()** of **fd2** returns an **ERR**, a "trouble reading" error message is displayed and the program aborts through the call to **exit(ERR)**. If the call to **write()** returns a value that is not equal to **num_byte** (i.e., the number of bytes read), a "trouble writing" message is displayed. The program then aborts through the call to **exit(ERR)**.

If both error checks are passed, the data is written to the disk. The **while** loop continues in this manner until the **read()** of **fd2** finds an end-of-file. Because **EOF** evaluates to zero, the **while** loop terminates. A check on the call to **close(fd1)** for the new file is made to make sure all went well. A call to **close(fd2)** frees up the file descriptor and closes the source file. A bell sounds, a message appears, and the program ends.

Try running the program in Figure 8.11 for a given file and time how long it takes. Then try to copy the same file with the copy utility provided with your operating system, again recording the time. Having done that, change **BUFF** to a single character variable and copy the same file again. What happened to the copy time? How does the C program compare to the system copy utility time (which is usually written in assembler)?

Other Alternatives

All of the examples we have seen in this chapter relied on reading and writing data in a sequential manner. That is, the file was opened, then we began reading/writing the data from the beginning of the file to its end. It is like a tape recording where all activity is referenced from the beginning of the tape.

As anyone who has ever worked with such storage devices knows, finding a given piece of data by a sequential read can be a very slow process. For example, let's suppose that you need a piece of information that is located 500 bytes from the beginning of the file. Sequential files force you to start at the beginning of the file and read through it to the data you want. As a result, you waste time reading 499 bytes of "unwanted" data.

Random access files, on the other hand, allow you to move about within the file as you see fit; you can go immediately to the desired information without reading the intervening data. Access time is substantially improved.

C provides for random access techniques with data files. It assumes, however, that you know where you want to be in the file. The `lseek()` function places us at a given location in a file and has the following general form:

```
lseek(file_descriptor, offset, base);
```

in which (1) `file_descriptor` is the integer number obtained from the call to `open()`, (2) `offset` is a `long` integer variable that contains the number of bytes to be positioned from the base, and (3) `base` is an integer variable that specifies the position in the file that will be used as the base position.

There are three possible values for `base`. If `base` equals `0`, the beginning of the file becomes the reference point. If `base` equals `1`, the current position in the file becomes the reference point. If `base` equals `2`, the end of the file is the reference point. Let's look at some examples.

Figure 8.12

`lseek(fd1, -1L, 1)`	places us one byte towards the beginning of the file. It "ungets" a byte. A negative `offset` moves us towards the beginning of the file.
`lseek(fd1, 0L, 0)`	places us at the beginning of the file.
`lseek(fd1, 0L, 2)`	places us at the end of the file.

We can make some generalizations from these examples. First, a negative value for `offset` when `base is 0` is an error. It suggests an attempt to place ourselves "in front of" the beginning of the file. Similarly, a `base` of `2` with a positive `offset` suggests that we're trying to go beyond the end-of-file, which is also an error. Therefore, `offset` cannot be negative when `base` is `0`, and `offset` cannot be positive when `base` is `2`. Depending on the current position in the file, positive and negative values for `offset` are valid when `base` equals `1`.

The **lseek()** function returns a value of zero if all is well and a negative value if an error occurred. Variations do exist, so you should check your documentation to see what is returned.

After the call to **lseek()** has positioned the pointer in the file, a read or write can be performed in the standard manner.

Those libraries that provide an **lseek()** function probably also provide a **tell()** function. The general form is

```
tell(fd1);
```

which returns a **long int** that is the current byte position in the file. If you get lost in a file, **tell()** "tells" you where you are relative to the beginning of the file. A negative value indicates an error.

Check your documentation for deviations. If the source code for your library is available, examine it to see how the high-level file I/O functions are implemented. You can learn a great deal by taking the time to study them.

Appendix 8
A Closer Look at File I/O

This Appendix provides details about file I/O that were not covered in Chapter 8. The CP/M operating system is assumed in those areas where specifics about the DOS are needed. With UNIX, much of the "clutter" of the operating system disappears because direct calls to the operating system are possible. Given the growing interest in C by those using CP/M, however, CP/M is the system used in the following discussion.

The FILE Structure

The form used for the **FILE** structure declaration is frequently the one shown in Figure 8A.1.

Figure 8A.1

```
typedef struct _buffer {
    int _fd;              /* file descriptor            */
    int _cleft;           /* characters left in buffer  */
    int _mode;            /* how you will work with file */
    char *_nextc;         /* location of next character */
    char *_buff;          /* location of buffer         */
} FILE;

    extern FILE _efile[_MAXFILE]
```

189

If we suppose that _MAXFILE equals 10, then we have an array of 10 structures like the one declared above. Therefore, the elements of the array _efile[0] through _efile[9] are available to the programmer and may be used with a disk file.

When the high-level disk I/O functions were used in Chapter 8, each program had a declaration similar to:

```
FILE *f1;
```

which declares the pointer variable f1 to point to a structure of type FILE. As with any other pointer variable, f1 points to "garbage" until it is initialized. To initialize f1 to point to something meaningful, we can use a statement similar to that in Figure 8A.2,

Figure 8A.2

```
if ((f1 = fopen(fname, "w")) == NULL) {
       .
       .
}
```

This statement initializes f1 to point to a previously unused element of _efile[]. The call to fopen() checks for an unused element in _efile[]. If one is available, fopen() returns a pointer to that element. That is, after a successful fopen(), f1 has an rvalue which points to an element of _efile[] and maintains the "overhead" information about the file and its status.

What is less obvious is that the high-level fopen() call actually goes through a low-level open() call to do this. To make this more concrete, examine Figure 8A.3.

Figure 8A.3

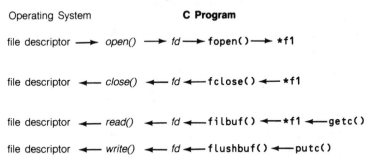

Operating System   C Program

file descriptor ⟶ *open()* ⟶ *fd* ⟶ fopen() ⟶ *f1

file descriptor ⟵ *close()* ⟵ *fd* ⟵ fclose() ⟵ *f1

file descriptor ⟵ *read()* ⟵ *fd* ⟵ filbuf() ⟵ *f1 ⟵ getc()

file descriptor ⟵ *write()* ⟵ *fd* ⟵ flushbuf() ⟵ putc()

Every disk operating system must provide the four disk I/O functions shown in Figure 8A.3 (i.e., **open**, **close**, **read**, and **write**). Some operating systems may also provide a **create** function if it is not part of the **fopen()** call.

Only a certain number of open files are allowed at one time. When you use an **fopen()** call, it calls **open()** and causes the operating system to check whether it has any unused file descriptors available. (Under CP/M, it looks for a file control block.)

The operating system looks for the first "unused" element in the array, then assigns the file you are trying to open to this unused element. A file descriptor is passed back to your program and used to keep track of which file belongs to what element in the operating system's array. Think of the file descriptor as the element position in the "available and used" array maintained by the operating system.

After the file descriptor is returned from the operating system, it is placed in the _fd member of the **FILE** structure. The **fopen()** function then passes back a pointer (e.g., *f1) to the element in the _efile[] array which is used to keep track of the file you just opened. Note how **fopen()** actually "passes through" **open()** to get the file pointer. In the process, it receives a file descriptor (**fd**) which is given to **fopen()**. Then **fopen()** gives you a file pointer (**f1**) after it returns from the operating system. In reality, therefore, *the operating system only uses* **fd** *to communicate with your program.*

Figure 8A.4 illustrates this process. In this example, we have as-

sumed that the operating system has an array of 10 available files
(_fcb[]) and that it selects the sixth one (i.e., actually _fcb[5]) to
assign to the file you are trying to open. The operating system is on
the left side of the figure, and your program is on the right.

Figure 8A.4

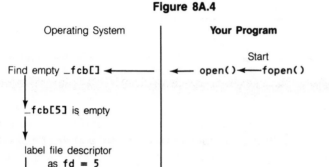

Your program attempts to open a file, which causes the operating
system to look for an "unused" file. If the operating system finds
_fcb[5] available, it passes back to your program the number **5** as
the file descriptor. *The file descriptor becomes the communications
link between your program and the operating system.* What **fopen()**
actually receives is a pointer to **fd**. From now on, your program will
"talk" with the operating system about this file by using the file
descriptor **5**. However, when you use the **fopen()**, **fclose()**,
putc(), and **getc()** functions in your programs, the statements
must use **fp**.

Communications with Files

Refer back to Figure 8A.3 for a moment and note how **getc()**
works. When you ask for a character from a file, **getc()** uses **fd** as
its argument and looks at the _cleft member of **FILE** to see if
another character is in the buffer. If there is another character, it is
returned. If not, a function named **filbuf()** goes to the operating
system to "refill" the buffer (and updates the _cleft and _nextc

members of **FILE**). The **putc()** function works in much the same manner, but reverses the direction of flow.

stdin, stdout, and stderr

The functions **getchar()** and **putchar()** work in much the same way. Let's consider **getchar()** first. You already know that this function gets a single character from the keyboard. If **getchar()** works through the mechanism described above (which it does), how does it get a character from the keyboard rather than a file?

Somewhere (often in one of the library routines) you will find a declaration similar to:

Figure 8A.5

```
#define stdin      (&_efile[0])
#define stdout     (&_efile[1])
#define stderr     (&_efile[2])
         .
         .
#define getchar()  getc(stdin)
#define putchar()  putc(c, stdout)
```

When **getchar()** is called, it calls **getc()** with **stdin** (standard input) as its argument. The operating system uses this element in the **_efile[]** array to access the keyboard because of the way **_efile[0]** was initialized. Similarly, **putchar()** calls **putc()** with the character **c** and **stdout** (standard output) as its arguments. Because of the way **_efile[1]** was initialized, output normally goes to the screen. If an error occurs, **stderr** (standard error) normally directs output to the screen.

If you dig around deep enough, you should find the initialization of **stdin**, **stdout**, and **stderr**. It should look like:

Figure 8A.6

```
FILE _efile[_MAXFILE] = {
     ( 0, 0, _CONIN, NULL, NULL),   /* standard input  */
     ( 1, 0, _CONOUT, NULL, NULL),  /* standard output */
     ( 2, 0, _CONOUT, NULL, NULL),  /* standard error  */
};
```

Referring back to the declaration of the **FILE** structure, you can see how each member is initialized. In terms of the CP/M environment, **_CONIN** (i.e., character in) and **_CONOUT** (i.e., character out) are standard references to the CP/M "jump table." You can change these initialized assignments to "redirect" the inputs and outputs to other devices (e.g., a printer).

Finally, Figure 8A.6 also suggests that the first three "files" provided by the operating system are "dedicated" to **stdin**, **stdout**, and **stderr**. Therefore, if your operating system has a limit on the maximum number of files that can be used at one time, the actual number available to you is three less than the maximum because of the requirements of **stdin**, **stdout**, and **stderr**.

Chapter 9
Common Mistakes and Debugging

C is not an easy language to learn. On the other hand, it is easier than some other languages (e.g., assembler). Let's examine some of the common mistakes that beginning C programmers make, pointing out what probably went wrong. We'll also look at some techniques you can use to debug your programs.

Common Mistakes

As with any language, the first level of program errors stems from not obeying the syntax rules of the language. Fortunately, these errors are the easiest to find. The compiler does most of the work.

Missing or Misplaced Semicolon

It may take you a while to get used to the idea of placing a semicolon at the end of a program statement. For example,

```
printf("\nThis is a mistake")
```

obviously needs a semicolon after the closing parentheses of the `printf()` function call. The compiler should catch this error.

Some compilers, however, generate "misleading" error messages in such cases. As the compiler scans (or "parses") the input line, it must check the syntax to see if a valid C construct has been used. If a semicolon is left out, the compiler will parse the *next* line as though it were part of the line with the missing semicolon. Depending on what is contained in the offending line as well as in the following line, the compiler may generate misleading error messages.

If the compiler says an error occurred in a given line and subsequent inspection of that line shows no errors, check the line before it for a missing semicolon. With some compilers, a missing semicolon in one line causes the compiler to "get lost" in the code. As a result, a series of error messages are given. In one case, a program had 46 errors. Once a single missing semicolon was found and corrected, the program compiled with no further errors.

Another common mistake is to place a semicolon where you really don't want one. For example,

```
for(i = 0; i < MAX; ++i);                    /* trouble! */
    x += 2;
```

This code was probably intended to increment variable **x** **MAX** times. However, as the code is written, **x** is incremented by two only one time. The way this line executes becomes clearer when it is written as

```
for(i = 0; i < MAX; ++i)
    ;
x += 2;
```

It should be obvious that this is a "do nothing" loop. The statement controlled by the **for** loop is a null statement (i.e., a lone semicolon). Such errors are worse than syntax errors because the code will compile and execute; it just doesn't execute properly. Similar mistakes can creep into other loops and conditional statements (e.g., **do-while**, **while**, and **if**).

Missing Braces

Forgetting to supply an opening or closing brace is another common mistake. The brace is normally used to group two or more statements together so they can be treated as a single statement. (Using braces for structures, unions, and initializing variables is less common.) If you forget to use braces when multiple statements are to be treated together, only the first program statement will be executed as planned. For example,

Figure 9.1

Wrong!	Intended

```
while (i < MAX)              while (i < MAX) {
    x[i] = func1();              x[i] = func1();
    ++i;                         ++i;
                             }
```

The program is probably meant to stuff the **x[]** array with some value returned from the call to **func1()**. Because braces are not used, however, only one element of **x[]** is assigned. In addition, if only one brace is supplied, mysterious things can happen, depending on the subsequent code.

Typically, a programmer may forget to supply matching braces when a loop construct is used with complex **if** statements. The compiler will catch this error, but may not tell you whether an opening or closing brace is the problem. As a dangerous generality, you are more likely to forget the closing brace.

The program in Figure 9.2 performs a simple brace count, looking for a match between opening and closing braces. Although this program cannot tell you where the extra or missing brace is, it is useful as a "precompile" step to check complex code where you think you may have a missing brace. It will probably execute faster than a compiler pass.

Figure 9.2

```
/* program to check opening and closing braces */
/* assumes that filename to be checked */
/* is a command line argument */

#include "stdio.h"
#define CLEARS 12               /* control codes for ADDS */
#define CURSOR "\033Y"          /* Viewpoint terminal */

main(argc, argv)
int argc;
char **argv;
{
     char last_char;
     int o_count, c_count, c;
     FILE *f1;

     putchar(CLEARS);
     if((f1 = fopen(argv[1], "r")) == NULL){
          printf("Can't open %s\n", argv[1]);
          exit(1);
     }
```

```
            last_char = ' ';
            o_count = c_count = 0;
            puts("Opening Braces        Closing Braces\n");
            while((c = getc(f1)) != EOF){
                if(last_char == '/' && c == '*'){
                    while(c != '/' && last_char != '*'){
                        last_char = c;
                        c = getc(f1);
                    }
                }
                if(c == '\''){
                    last_char = c;
                    c = getc(f1);
                    if(c == '\\'){
                        while(c != '\'')
                            c = getc(f1);
                    }
                    if(c == '{' || c == '}')
                        c = getc(f1);
                }
                if(c == '"' && last_char != '\"'){
                    c = getc(f1);
                    while(c != '"')
                        c = getc(f1);
                }
                if(c == '{'){
                    o_count += 1;
                    set_cur(2,7, o_count);
                }
                if(c == '}'){
                    c_count += 1;
                    set_cur(2, 30, c_count);
                }
                last_char = c;
            }
        fclose(f1);
        if((o_count - c_count) == 0)
            printf("\n\nBrace count is okay!!!\n");
        else
            printf("\n\nBrace count is incorrect.\n");
    }
set_cur(row, col, num)
int row, col, num;
{
    printf("%s%c%c%d", CURSOR, row+31, col+31, num);
}
```

This program is fairly simple, but a few comments are warranted. The variable `last_char` lets us check for program comments, quoted strings, and single characters that may contain a brace. When the compiler senses a `/*` character pair, a double, or a single quotation mark, the program will "waste" characters until a matching `*/`, ', or " is read.

The rest of the program keeps track of opening and closing braces. If the brace counts don't match, the user is informed. Given the higher probability of forgetting a closing brace, the brace counts can help you find the missing or extra brace.

Assignment versus Relational Test

It is easy to forget a double-equal sign when you perform a relational test. Depending on the context in which the double-equal sign is used, the compiler may or may not catch it as an obvious error. (You may want to try a = in a program where a = = should be used to see how your compiler handles the double-equal sign.) Consider the following type of error:

Figure 9.3

Wrong!	Intended
`for (i = 0; i = MAX; ++i)`	`for (i = 0; i == MAX; ++i)`

The middle expression in a `for` loop usually involves some form of test between two variables. In the example above, we have tried to *assign* i to equal `MAX`. These mistakes are typically just annoyances that are revealed during compilation.

Other assignment errors can be more subtle, however. The following valid assignment

```
flag = start = end = x = 0;
```

sets each variable to equal zero. Now consider

```
flag = array[i] == 'x';
```

which is also a valid statement, but with an entirely different meaning. This statement says: If the character `array[i]` equals the character x, then the relation `array[i] == 'x'` is logic True, so *assign* `flag` to equal 1 (i.e., logic True). This statement works the way it does because the precedence of the relational operator (= =) is higher than that of assignment.

The same results can be obtained with the more conventional

```
flag = (array[i] == 'x') ? 1 : 0;
```

Although the ternary operator makes this statement clearer, the other form is also valid. Experiment with the relational and assignment operators to verify the above.

Program Comments

The /* and */ characters introduce comments into a program. Because the compiler strips away everything in between these characters, you can make liberal use of comments in a program. They have no effect on the size or speed of the compiled program. Be sure to use them carefully, however.

A friend of mine was compiling a very complex program that involved a large number of functions which were not part of the common library. He painstakingly documented each function, including a heading that looked something like that in Figure 9.4.

Figure 9.4

```
/**********************************************************/
/*                    func1(*x, *y, *z)                 */
/*   (Herein began a rather lengthy description of what the */
/*     the function was designed to do....)             */
/**********************************************************
```

When he tried to link everything together, several of the functions would not link properly. After much head scratching, we noticed that the trailing slash was missing in one of the headings, just as in the figure above.

In this particular case, several functions that immediately followed **func1()** had no comments. Because the compiler "throws away" everything between the opening /* and the companion */, it kept reading the missing functions as comments until it finally found a closing */. If there had been no further comments in the file, the compiler would probably have given us an "unexpected end-of-file" message. This would have made it easier to find the error.

You may want to reproduce this error on your compiler to see what error message, if any, is given. It's easier to figure out what went wrong when you see the error message under "controlled" conditions.

The first four types of errors are fairly common, and you should expect your fair share; it is part of learning C. Errors, however, have a way of growing right along with you. As you gain experience, the errors you make also gain a level of sophistication. Generally, these errors are not caught by the compiler. The program compiles and links properly, but the results aren't correct.

It's at this point that raw perseverance comes into play. Let's proceed to level two.

Arguments to Functions are Copies

Any time you pass a variable to a function, a copy of the variable is made. To preserve the integrity of variables between functions, the function does *not* receive the actual variable. By making variables local, or private, to the function, there is less chance of interaction between functions. (If this seems fuzzy, review Chapter 4.)

Array and pointer variables are exceptions to this rule. You can change the original value of a variable only if you purposely pass the address of the variable to the function. When an array is passed to a function, it receives the address of the array. (Specifically, it receives the address of element zero in the array.)

One common mistake is to use an argument in the following manner:

Figure 9.5

```
main()
{
     .
     .
     cube(x);
     printf("\nThe cube is %d", x);
     .
}
cube(x)
int x;
{
     x = x * x * x;
     return (x);
}
```

In this example, the programmer passed a copy of **x** to **cube( )** and expected **x** to reflect the new value after the function call. However, because the variable **x** in **cube( )** is a copy that "dies" when you leave the function, it has no way of changing **x** in **main( )**. Only by using a pointer can this program function properly. That is, we would have to pass the *address* of x to the function by using **cube(&x)**. We would also have to modify the **cube( )** function as follows:

Figure 9.6

```
cube(x)
int *x;
{
     *x = *x * *x * *x;
}
```

As a general rule, *use a pointer only when you want a function call to alter the original value of the argument to the function.* If the function can do its job by using a copy of the argument, don't use a pointer. If a pointer is not used, don't expect the function to alter the value of an argument that is passed to it.

Keep in mind that arrays passed as arguments to a function do pass the address of the array. *Passing the name of an array variable is the same as using a pointer.*

Forgetting to Declare Arguments in a Function Call

Consider the following skeletal program.

Figure 9.7

```
main()
{
     char let[MAX];

     .
     .
     func1(let);
     .
}
func1(s)
{
     .
     .
     .
}
```

In this situation, we wanted to pass the character array let[] to func1() to alter the contents of the array in some way. However, because the array is received as variable s in func1() and is not explicitly declared, s defaults to an int. Undeclared arguments in a function call are ints by default.

The actual code in func1() would play a large part in determining how tough this error would be to find and how much help the compiler would be in locating it.

Make sure that you declare all arguments in a function call, including integer variables.

Forgetting to Declare Functions in main()

Just as undeclared arguments to a function default to an int, so does whatever is returned from a function. For example, consider the skeletal program in Figure 9.8.

Figure 9.8

```
main()
{
    double bignum;

    bignum = func1(bignum);
    printf("\nThe answer is %e", bignum);
        .
}
func1(dbl)
double dbl;
{
        .
        .
    return (dbl);
}
```

So what's the problem? When the **return (dbl)** is executed, the value returned is an **int** because **func1()** is a function that returns an **int** by default. A step in the right direction would be to declare **func1()** to return a **double**. The function should be

Figure 9.9

```
double func1(dbl)
double dbl;
{
        .
        .
    return(dbl);
}
```

Now the function is set up to return a **double** to **main()**. Unfortunately, we've only solved half the problem.

Function Calls Return Integers to main()

As you know, the default data type passed to a function is an **int**. Any arguments other than integers must state their data type in the argument declarations. The same logic applies in the other direction: anything returned from a function defaults to an **int**. Although we corrected **func1()** to return a **double** to **main()** through the

double func1() function declaration, **main()** still thinks that it is getting an integer back from **func1()**. To let **main()** in on **func1()**'s secret, the function name must be declared to return a **double** in **main()**. The proper form is shown in Figure 9.10.

Figure 9.10

```
main()
{
     double bignum, func1();   /* now main() knows */

        .
        .
}
double func1(dbl)
double dbl;
{
        .
        .
}
```

Now both **func1()** and **main()** are declared to handle the **double** properly. If a function will return something other than an **int**, two rules must be followed: (1) the data type must precede the function name in the function definition, and (2) the function name must be declared with the appropriate data type in **main()**.

Another solution would be to declare **func1()** before **main()** because function names are globally available to the rest of the program. The **main()** would then know that the function returns a **double**.

On a related topic, remember that **chars** are promoted to **ints** during a function call, and that **floats** are promoted to **doubles**. If you plan to do a lot of number-crunching calls to functions using **floats**, it may be faster to do everything simply with **doubles**. If you use **doubles**, you can bypass the conversion of the **float** to **double** before the function call.

The same is true of math operations on **floats**. Because math operations are done in double precision, to use **floats** you must convert to **double**, do the math operation, then convert back to **float**.

When you use **doubles** instead of **floats**, you skip two conversion steps.

A Pointer Contains Garbage Until it is Initialized

If you try to use a pointer before you assign it to a variable address, it will undoubtedly *not* point to anything useful. The rule is simple: *always initialize a pointer before you use it.*

Another thing to remember about pointers is that when an array variable is passed to a function, the array variable behaves like a pointer in that the function receives a pointer to the array. The reverse does not work, however. If you declare an array in a function, you cannot pass a pointer back to **main()** for subsequent work on the array created in the function. All variables defined in a function have an **auto** storage class and disappear when the function is exited. Their contents are lost outside the function.

Plain Stupidity

Some errors have a way of becoming a challenge and lead to a sense of satisfaction when they are uncovered. Others are just plain stupid. You know better, and the error is so obvious that you don't see it. These errors come under the ''it's-time-to-go-to-bed'' category. The program in Figure 9.11 is a good (?) example of a stupid mistake I made while writing this book. Take a moment or two to find the error before you continue reading.

Figure 9.11

```
#include "stdio.h"
#define CLEARS '\014'
#define MAX 200

main(argc, argv)
int argc;
char **argv;
```

```
{
    FILE *fp;
    char c, let[MAX];
    int i, x, j;

    putc(CLEARS);
    if ((fp = fopen(argv[1], "r")) == NULL) {
        printf("\nCan't open file %s", argv[1]);
        exit(1);
    }

    puts("The purpose of this program is to...");
    .
    .
}
```

Although the error may be obvious to you, it wasn't to me at the time.

Now that you have studied the program, take a close look at the **putc(CLEARS)** function call. Obviously, I wanted to clear the screen before printing a message to the user. That is, I should have used **putchar(CLEARS)** instead of **putc()**. I was trying to write to a file that wasn't opened yet. In my case, the program simply "went west" (i.e., the poetic term for locking up the system).

Because the program involved several different data files, I assumed that something was wrong in the (more complex) code which dealt with the file I/O. It was only after I had checked through the file I/O section completely that I saw the error.

Note: The functions **getc()** and **putc()** work with files, whereas **getchar()** and **putchar()** are usually relegated to the screen and keyboard. Operating systems may vary, and other possibilities exist. (See the Appendix to Chapter 8.)

Such errors do occur and can be very difficult to find because you refuse to believe that you could make a dumb mistake. There's a tendency to assume that there must be a complex reason for the error, particularly as you gain experience with the language. If an error is difficult to find, it's probably time to take a break. A few minutes away from the code can make even the most well-concealed error obvious.

Debugging

Someone once called a "bug" an undocumented feature of a program. Regardless of what it's called, an error is an error and must be isolated and corrected. There are three fundamental steps in this process: (1) detecting the error, (2) isolating the error, and (3) correcting the error. The first two steps are the most difficult.

Kinds of Errors

Syntax Errors

The easiest errors to detect are those we discussed at the beginning of this chapter. Syntax errors fall into this category. In most cases, the compiler will both detect and isolate the error for you. Most compilers will also tell you the line number in the source program where the error occurred. Error correction is reduced to editing the source file and recompiling it. Such syntax errors fall into the "dumb mistake" category and are easy to correct.

Program Errors

The more serious type of error is one that goes undetected by the compiler and results in a program that executes, but produces the wrong results. In this case, the source of the error must be detected and isolated by the programmer. Error correction is still fairly simple because you know an error exists in the program. Detection of the error is simple: the results of the program are incorrect. Isolating the error is usually the most difficult aspect of debugging in these situations.

Latent Bugs

The most pernicious bug is the "latent bug"—one that lies dormant during testing, but shows up only when a certain data set is supplied to the program. The most difficult aspect of the latent bug is detecting the error. Once the data set that caused the error is known, isolation and correction of the error are usually fairly simple.

C can be made less error prone than many languages, especially BASIC, provided that you understand C's strong points. The privacy given to data through function calls minimizes the unwanted side effects that interaction between variables can produce.

There is a tendency, however, for beginning programmers to defeat this inherent protection by avoiding function calls. Because they are uncomfortable with how functions work (e.g., pointers in particular), they tend to place code that should be a function call in **main()**. Unfortunately, when you place all of the data in **main()**, you make it available to other elements in the program; therefore, error isolation becomes more difficult.

A preventative measure to lessen the need for debugging is *defensive coding*, which means pushing the busy work out of **main()** into function calls. When you use function calls to do the busy work, you minimize interactions between variables. The fewer the data manipulations in **main()**, the less likely the chance of contaminating other data in the program. This is also an argument for keeping external storage class variables to a minimum. The greater the privacy afforded to the data, the easier it will be to isolate the error in the debugging process.

Most programs are composed of a series of smaller tasks, or intermediate steps, that build up to a final result. Each small task is probably a candidate for a function call. "Divide and conquer" has real meaning in C; push the busy work out of **main()** if possible. Divide and separate the work into smaller, more manageable, function calls.

Outlining the program and its underlying algorithm in a pseudo-language form is beneficial because it makes the smaller tasks readily identifiable. Once the individual tasks are known, each can be coded as a function call and tested separately. If errors do occur, at least you will have a smaller section of code to examine.

Error Detection and Isolation

Error detection is done by the compiler, the programmer, and (sadly) the user. The compiler can detect syntactic and semantic errors. It cannot, of course, detect a properly coded, but faulty, algorithm. With programming experience, compiler errors tend to disappear.

The more difficult error is one where the program executes, but does not produce the desired results. In these situations, the programmer must check through the code for the error. (We are assuming that the algorithm is correct.)

The process of error detection begins with a set of check data (data that are known to be correct). The known data is fed into the program, and the program is "divided down" until the source of the error is isolated. Dividing down the program consists of placing various `printf()` statements in the program to see intermediate results. Although a lone `printf()` will do, the function in Figure 9.12 is a suggested alternative.

Figure 9.12

```
/* function to print ints, chars, and numeric-character arrays */

debug(let, c_array, narray, asize, num, opt)
int num, narray[], opt, asize;
char let, c_array[];
{
     int i;

     switch (opt) {

          case 1:
               printf("\nThe value is %d", num);
               break;

          case 2:
               printf("\nThe letter is: %c", let);
               break;

          case 3:
               puts("\nThe numeric array contains\n");
               for (i = 0; i <= asize; ++i)
                    printf(" %d", narray[i]);
               break;

          case 4:
               puts("\nThe character array contains\n");
               for (i = 0; i <= asize; ++i)
                    printf(" %c", c_array[i]);
               break;

          default:
               puts("\nInvalid option selected.");
               break;

     }

     puts("\n\tPress any key to continue: ");
     getchar();
}
```

The **debug()** function gives you an easy way to print out common information used in the debugging process. (If your compiler supports other data types, they can be put into the function before the **default** case.)

Although the **debug()** function is overkill for simple integer and character variables, it can save time when arrays are used. In these cases, more than a simple **printf()** is needed if you want to look at the array (e.g., look at **cases 3** and **4** in Figure 9.12). Because the function is available, however, cases for printing out integer and character variables were included.

The idea of **debug()** is simple: Pass it the data type to be printed, and a subsequent **case** statement prints it out. The call to **getchar()** causes the program to pause until you press a key to continue. The argument list includes everything you need to make the function work. That is,

```
debug(let, c_array, narray, asize, num, opt)
```

in which **let** is a single character, **c_array** is a character array, **narray** is an integer array, **asize** is the number of elements to be printed in the array, **num** is an integer value, and **opt** is the option that you want to use. The code in the **debug()** function is simple and doesn't need elaboration.

Figure 9.13 is a simple program that can be used to test the **debug()** function call. The comments suggest what data type is being passed to the **debug()** function. Note that the preprocessor directive **#include** is used to include the **debug()** function in the program. As an alternative, we could delete the **#include** and link the function in as a separate module.

Figure 9.13

```
#define CLEARS 12                      /* clears my screen */
#include "debug.c"

main()
{
     int i, x, val[5];
     char alpha, let[5];

                                       /* put in some sample data */
     for (i = 65, x = 0; i < 70 ; ++i, ++x) {
          val[x] = x;
          let[x] = i;
     }

     putchar(CLEARS);

     alpha = 'z';

     debug(0, 0, 0, 0, i, 1);        /* display value */
     debug(alpha, 0, 0, 0, 0, 2);    /* display letter */
     debug(0, 0, val, 5, 0, 3);      /* display numeric array */
     debug(0, let, 0, 5, 0, 4);      /* display char array */
     debug(0, 0, 0, 0, 0, 7);        /* error */

}
```

The first call to **debug( )** asks that the integer value of variable **i** be displayed, which you can see by looking at the argument list in **debug( )**. The variable **num** receives a copy of **i**, and **opt** receives a **1**. **case 1** then prints out the value of **i** and pauses the program while we look at it.

In the second call to **debug( )**, a **char** variable (**alpha**) is passed using option 2. **cases 1** and **2** require only two arguments: the variable to be displayed and the option number.

The third and fourth calls to **debug( )** pass the number of elements of the array to be displayed. If you think it may be useful, you can add another argument to **debug( )** and pass the starting and ending elements to be printed. The last call simply shows what happens when the **default** is executed. If your compiler supports other data types, they also can be added to **debug( )**.

In many cases, you will have a good idea as to what is causing an error. In those situations, you may want to use a simple **printf( )**

rather than **debug()**. When working with arrays, however, **debug()** is simpler.

Finally, **debug()** has one other important advantage. After you have found and corrected the error, you can easily remove all occurrences of the **debug()** function call. Most text editors have a "search" facility that quickly finds all calls to **debug()**. Removing those calls and the **#include** for **debug()** is much easier than plowing through a bunch of **printf()**s and trying to decide which ones should be removed and which should stay (plus any other code needed to print out the debugging information, as with arrays).

One final suggestion is that you try using for each new program extreme values for the data. Things may look fine until the data are stretched to the limit. For example, consider a subcalculation in statistics where the sums-of-squares of two variables are multiplied together, then the square root of the product is taken:

```
i_val = sqr(sum_sq_x * sum_sq_y);
```

Code similar to this worked for three years without failing in a program used by several thousand users. Then someone plugged in a very large data set by using Gross National Product (in dollars) for both variables. The program failed. The correction was simple: taking the square root of the numbers *before* multiplying them.

The (latent) bug was there all the time, but it never showed up until the data were pushed to their limit. Machine overflow and underflow are always potential problems. The best you can hope to do is to minimize the chance of their occurring.

Some Concluding Thoughts

If you have gotten this far, it's probably because you recognize the power and advantages offered by C. As you gain experience with C, you will become even more convinced. And a growing number of people agree with you. Although C is not perfect, it is a lot better than many of the alternatives.

This text used simple examples to convey the fundamentals of the C programming language. Now that you're ready to set out on your own, you will need more complex examples to study. There are many subtleties of C that we have not covered in this book. One way of discovering them is to examine the code of other C programmers.

To that end, I strongly urge you to join the C Users' Group. The nominal cost (presently $10.00 per year) includes a subscription to their newsletter. Equally important, they have a growing library of C programs that are available for a nominal copying charge (less than $10.00 per volume, including the disk!). The programs on these disks are a great source for learning new coding techniques. There are also other benefits. For further information, write to

C Users' Group
P.O.Box 287
Yates Center, Kansas   66783

Who knows, before long *you* may be contributing programs to their library.

Appendix A
ASCII Codes

The codes for the American Standard for Coded Information Interchange, or ASCII, are listed below. These codes are given for those numbering systems commonly used in C. A control character is indicated by ∧; a Control-C is shown as ∧C.

Table A.1

Decimal	Hex	Octal	Binary	ASCII
0	00	000	00000000	null (NUL)
1	01	001	00000001	∧A (SOH)
2	02	002	00000010	∧B (STX)
3	03	003	00000011	∧C (ETX)
4	04	004	00000100	∧D EOT
5	05	005	00000101	∧E ENQ
6	06	006	00000110	∧F ACK
7	07	007	00000111	∧G (bell) BEL
8	08	010	00001000	∧H (backspace) BS
9	09	011	00001001	∧I (tab) horizontal HT
10	0A	012	00001010	∧J (linefeed) LF
11	0B	013	00001011	∧K (vertical tabs) VT
12	0C	014	00001100	∧L (formfeed) FF
13	0D	015	00001101	∧M (carriage return) CR
14	0E	016	00001110	∧N SO
15	0F	017	00001111	∧O SI
16	10	020	00010000	∧P DLE

Decimal	Hex	Octal	Binary	ASCII
17	11	021	00010001	∧Q DC1
18	12	022	00010010	∧R DC2
19	13	023	00010011	∧S DC3
20	14	024	00010100	∧T (DC4)
21	15	025	00010101	∧U (NAK)
22	16	026	00010110	∧V (SYN)
23	17	027	00010111	∧W (ETB)
24	18	030	00011000	∧X (CAN)
25	19	031	00011001	∧Y (EM)
26	1A	032	00011010	∧Z (SUB)
27	1B	033	00011011	Escape
28	1C	034	00011100	FS
29	1D	035	00011101	GS
30	1E	036	00011110	RS
31	1F	037	00011111	US
32	20	040	00100000	Space
33	21	041	00100001	!
34	22	042	00100010	'
35	23	043	00100011	#
36	24	044	00100100	$
37	25	045	00100101	%
38	26	046	00100110	&
39	27	047	00100111	'
40	28	050	00101000	(
41	29	051	00101001	)
42	2A	052	00101010	*
43	2B	053	00101011	+
44	2C	054	00101100	,
45	2D	055	00101101	-
46	2E	056	00101110	.
47	2F	057	00101111	/
48	30	060	00110000	0
49	31	061	00110001	1
50	32	062	00110010	2
51	33	063	00110011	3
52	34	064	00110100	4
53	35	065	00110101	5
54	36	066	00110110	6
55	37	067	00110111	7
56	38	070	00111000	8
57	39	071	00111001	9
58	3A	072	00111010	:
59	3B	073	00111011	;
60	3C	074	00111100	<
61	3D	075	00111101	=
62	3E	076	00111110	>

Decimal	Hex	Octal	Binary	ASCII
63	3F	077	00111111	?
64	40	100	01000000	@
65	41	101	01000001	A
66	42	102	01000010	B
67	43	103	01000011	C
68	44	104	01000100	D
69	45	105	01000101	E
70	46	106	01000110	F
71	47	107	01000111	G
72	48	110	01001000	H
73	49	111	01001001	I
74	4A	112	01001010	J
75	4B	113	01001011	K
76	4C	114	01001100	L
77	4D	115	01001101	M
78	4E	116	01001110	N
79	4F	117	01001111	O
80	50	120	01010000	P
81	51	121	01010001	Q
82	52	122	01010010	R
83	53	123	01010011	S
84	54	124	01010100	T
85	55	125	01010101	U
86	56	126	01010110	V
87	57	127	01010111	W
88	58	130	01011000	X
89	59	131	01011001	Y
90	5A	132	01011010	Z
91	5B	133	01011011	[
92	5C	134	01011100	\
93	5D	135	01011101	]
94	5E	136	01011110	^
95	5F	137	01011111	_
96	60	140	01100000	
97	61	141	01100001	a
98	62	142	01100010	b
99	63	143	01100011	c
100	64	144	01100100	d
101	65	145	01100101	e
102	66	146	01100110	f
103	67	147	01100111	g
104	68	150	01101000	h
105	69	151	01101001	i
106	6A	152	01101010	j
107	6B	153	01101011	k
108	6C	154	01101100	l

Decimal	Hex	Octal	Binary	ASCII
109	6D	155	01101101	m
110	6E	156	01101110	n
111	6F	157	01101111	o
112	70	160	01110000	p
113	71	161	01110001	q
114	72	162	01110010	r
115	73	163	01110011	s
116	74	164	01110100	t
117	75	165	01110101	u
118	76	166	01110110	v
119	77	167	01110111	w
120	78	170	01111000	x
121	79	171	01111001	y
122	7A	172	01111010	z
123	7B	173	01111011	{
124	7C	174	01111100	|
125	7D	175	01111101	}
126	7E	176	01111110	~
127	7F	177	01111111	del, rubout

Appendix B
Commercial C Compilers

This Appendix lists some of the moderately priced, commercially available C compilers. All of those listed are available for the CP/M operating system, unless otherwise noted. Some of these compilers are available for other operating systems. What follows is not an endorsement of any of the compilers listed, rather a source for further information. Write to the individual vendors for complete details before purchasing any compiler.

Some of the compilers listed are translations of the compiler (Small-C) written by Ron Cain and published in Vol. 45 of *Dr. Dobbs Journal* (DDJ) (Box E, 1263 El Camino Real, Menlo Park, CA, 94025). Small-C does not support the full set of operators and data types available in C. At a minimum, however, it does have **chars** and **ints**.

Note: *The Journal* has featured many interesting articles on C and will probably continue to do so. An updated version of Small-C appears in Volume 74 of *DDJ*.

If the full C language is supported, the compiler is described as "Complete C" below. A complete C compiler may or may not support bit fields.

Company	Target CPU or Machine	Comments
Caprock Systems, Inc. P.O. Box 13814 Arlington, TX 76013	IBM PC	A derivative of Small C. $35.00.
The Code Works P.O. Box 550 Goleta, CA 93116	8080 or Z80 CP/M	Several versions are available. Prices range from $19.95 (for Small-C) to $95.00 (an expanded Small-C).
Computer Innovations 75 Pine Street Lincroft, NJ 07738	IBM PC	Complete C. A nice implementation. $250.00.
Ecosoft, Inc. P.O. Box 68602 Indianapolis, IN 46268	Z80 CP/M IBM PC	Complete C. (IBM version in third quarter of 1983). A very nice implementation. $350.00.
InfoSoft Systems, Inc. 25 Sylvan Road South Westport, CT 06880	N/A	N/A
Lifeboat Associates 1651 Third Avenue New York, NY 10028	8080 or Z80 CP/M	Sells the BDS C compiler (no longs, floats, or doubles) for 8080-Z80 CP/M. $150.00.
Manx Software Systems P.O. Box 55 Shrewsbury, NJ 07701	8080 or Z80 CP/M	Sells Aztec C compiler for $200.00. Also available for Apple and IBM PC.
Software Toolworks 14478 Glorietta Dr. Sherman Oaks, CA 91423	8080 or Z80 CP/M	C/80 C compiler (no longs, floats, or doubles). $50.00.
Supersoft P.O. Box 1628 Champaign, IL 61820	8080 or Z80 CP/M	Supersoft C. $200.00.

tiny-C Associates P.O. Box 269 Holmdel, NJ 07733	8080 or Z80 CP/M	Sells a compiled and interpreter version. Very nice documentation. There are some deviations from standard C syntax. No floats or doubles. $100.00 to $250.00.
Telecon Systems 1155 Meridian Ave. San Jose, CA 95125	*	Sells several versions for a variety of operating systems. Prices range from $200.00 to $500.00.
Whitesmiths, Ltd. Parkway Towers, 'B' US Route 1 So. Iselin, NJ 08830	*	Complete C for several different operating systems. $750.00.
Dedicated Micro Systems, Inc. P.O. Box 287 112 N. Main Yates Center, KS 66783	8080 or Z80 CP/M	BDS C Compiler for $115.00 (see Lifeboat Assoc. above)

*8080-Z80 CP/M supported, plus other minicomputer operating systems.

Appendix C
Syntax Summary

This Appendix summarizes the fundamental syntax features of C in one place for easy reference, but is not intended as a replacement for the information in the text. However, this Appendix should prove helpful if you forget a syntax rule with a given statement (e.g., does a `for` loop use a comma or a semicolon, or both?). Where applicable, a short example is given.

Objects, Data Types, Identifiers, and Storage Classes

Objects

An object is an area of memory in which a specific type of data is stored. There are four fundamental types of objects: `char`, `int`, `float`, and `double`.

char

A `char` is an area of storage that is large enough to hold one element of the computer's character set.

For a microcomputer, the ASCII characters set (see Appendix A) normally uses 1 byte of storage. (An 8-bit byte is used even though an ASCII character only requires 7 bits.)

int

An **int** is an area of storage that holds an integer number.

Typically, **int** is twice as large as **char** (e.g., 2 bytes). Valid modifiers include the categories **short**, **long**, and **unsigned**.

float

A **float** is an area of storage that holds a single-precision, floating-point number.

Typically, **float** requires an area that is 4 times that of a **char** (e.g., 4 bytes).

double

A **double** is an area of storage that holds a double-precision, floating-point number.

Typically, a **double** requires twice as much storage as a **float** (e.g., 8 bytes).

Data Types

The four types of objects may combined into five derived data types:

1. Arrays of objects (e.g., an array of **chars**, or an array of **ints**).

2. Functions that may return an object (e.g., a function returning **int**).

3. Pointers to objects (e.g., a pointer to **ints**).

4. A structure that holds two or more objects (e.g., a structure of a **char**, an **int**, and an array of **floats**).

5. A **union** to store any size object. Only one object, however, can reside in the **union** at one time (e.g., a **union** of **char**, **int**, and **double**, but with only one of these objects in the **union** at a time).

Identifiers

An identifier is used to name an object. The name references the object in a program (e.g., variable and function names).

1. The letters A through Z (upper and lower case are different), the digits 0 through 9, and the underscore ("_").

2. The first character must be a letter or an underscore (not a digit).

3. Variable and function names may be as long as you wish, but no more than the first eight characters are significant. (Check the documentation on both the compiler and the linker. Several major linkers are limited to six characters of significance.)

Storage Classes

There are four storage classes: **auto**matic, **static**, **external**, and **register**.

Automatic

An **auto**matic storage class is an object whose value(s) are local to a function or block in a program, as in the following:

```
fctn()
{
    int x;
    x=7;
    while (1) {
        float x;
        fc2(&x);
        if(x==1.375)
        break;
    }
    printf("%d\n",x);
}
```

1. The keyword **auto** is reserved for the automatic storage class.

2. The value of an **auto** variable is not available outside the function or block in which it is declared (i.e., **auto** variables are not globally available throughout the program).

3. The value of an **auto** variable is lost on leaving the function or block.

4. Unless otherwise specified or declared outside any function or block, all objects are of the **auto** storage class.

Static

A **static** storage class is like **auto**, with the following exception:

The value that a variable had when the function was last exited is the value of the variable the next time the function or block is entered. For example, if variable **col_2** is 7 when the **cursor( )** function is exited, **col_2** has a starting value of 7 the next time **cursor( )** is called.

An **auto**, by contrast, will contain garbage on the second call to **cursor( )**; an **auto** variable "dies" on leaving the function.

External

External variables are globally available throughout the program. They have values that "live" throughout the program.

Register

A **register** is a variable that is stored in a register of the CPU. Typically, a **register** is used to store **char**, **int**, and pointer variables when execution speed is an important consideration in the program.

1. The data type cannot exceed the storage limitations of the register. That is, if the CPU has 16-bit registers, a (32-bit) **float** cannot be stored in a register.

2. **register** variables have an **auto** storage class.

3. You cannot take the address of a **register**.

4. Most compilers limit the number of **register** variables that can be used at one time. There is no guarantee that requesting a **register** storage class will actually result in the variable's being placed in a register. If no register is available, the object is placed in memory. The compiler will try to place the object in a register if one is available.

Attributes, lvalues, rvalues, Pointers, and Indirection

Attributes

Each identifier is of a specific type and storage class. The attributes of the identifier, therefore, are its type and storage class.

Collectively, the declaration of the identifier sets its attributes. For example,

```
register int i_loop;
```

declares the variable i_loop (i.e., the identifier) and is an integer variable of the register storage class.

lvalues and rvalues

Each object resides at an address in memory, which becomes its lvalue, and has something stored at that address, which is its rvalue. Therefore, the *lvalue is the object's address, and its rvalue is what the object contains.*

For example, let's suppose that the character 'A' has been assigned to a variable named let_r. Let's further assume that it has been stored at memory address 50,000 by the compiler. The lvalue of let_r is 50,000, and its rvalue is 'A'.

Pointers and Indirection

The rvalue of a pointer variable is the address of another variable of a specified type. Notice the following example:

```
char let_r, *ptr_let;

let_r = 'A';
ptr_let = &let_r;
```

Let's assume that let_r is an object of type char stored at address 50,000, and that ptr_let is a pointer to type char stored at address 60,000. The lvalue of ptr_let is 60,000, and its rvalue is 50,000. In this example, ptr_let points to the character 'A' through a process called indirection. That is,

```
printf("The character is %c", *ptr_let);
```

prints the character 'A' on the screen.

Expressions, Statements, and Braces

Expressions

An expression is a series of one or more operands connected by an operator. Some examples of expressions are

```
c = 25
y = (x * z) / n
y--
```

In the first example, the expression is the unary assignment operator, which assigns 25 to **c**. The second example involves three operators (multiplication, division, and assignment), whereas the third example uses only one operator (postdecrement). *Unary* operators (e.g., postdecrement) have one operand, *binary* operators (e.g., multiply) have two operands, and *ternary* operators (e.g., **x = (y = = TRUE) ? 1 : 0)** require three operands.

For complex expressions, the hierarchy of operators (see Chapter 7) determines the order in which the expression is evaluated. The precedence rules are strict, which is why an expression such as

```
x = y == 2
```

is a valid expression. Because the double-equal sign (i.e., test for equality) is of higher precedence than the single equal sign (i.e., assignment), the test for equality is performed first, then the assignment to **x**. What is assigned to **x**? If **y** equals 2, the expression is logic True, so **x** is assigned the value of 1. If **y** does not equal 2, the expression is logic False, and **x** is assigned to equal 0.

Statements and Braces

Any expression in C that is terminated by a semicolon is a *statement*. Therefore,

```
c = 25;
y = (x * z) / n;
```

```
y--;
```

are now statements, whereas they were simply expressions before.

Statements can be grouped together into a single, larger statement (also called compound statements or blocks) with braces. Therefore, anywhere a single statement can appear in C, multiple statements can be used if they are surrounded by braces. One common example is the **if** statement.

```
if (expression)              if (expression) {
    statement;                   statement one;
                                 statement two;
                                     .
                                 statement n;
                             }
```

If the **expression** is True, the statement is executed. In the example on the right, if **expression** is True, **statement** is again executed. In this situation, however, **statement** actually consists of **n** statements grouped together by braces. In other words, the use of braces in the second example forces the **if** to view the **n** statements as though they were a single statement.

Braces may contain multiple statements and declarations. They may also contain a single statement, but then they are redundant.

Keywords

Despite its power, C has relatively few keywords. They are

Keywords

Data Types	Storage Classes	Statements
char	auto	break
int	static	case
float	extern	continue
double	register	default
long		do
short		else
struct		for
union		goto
unsigned		if
		return
		sizeof
typedef		switch
		while
		(entry)

(The entry keyword is not yet implemented, and typedef is really not a storage class in itself, but rather a shorthand form for existing data types.)

Statement Keywords

In this section, expression is abbreviated as exp and followed by a number if the statement uses more than one expression. The abbreviation id is used for identifier.

for

```
for(exp1 ; exp2 ; exp3 )
     statement;
```

Typically, exp1 initializes one or more variables, expr2 performs a relational test, and expr3 increments or decrements a variable. For example,

```
for(i = 0; i < MAX; ++i)      for(i = 0, m = 1; m == 10;
     s[i] = i + OFFSET;             ++i, m++){
                                    sum[i] = i * m;
                                    sumsq *= sum[i];
                               }
```

In the second example, both i and m are initialized as part of exp1, then incremented as part of **exp3**. (Note the compound statement and multiple subexpressions.)

if-else

```
if (exp)                                 if(exp)
     statement;           or                      statement 1;
                                         else
                                                  statement 2;
```

If the **expression** that follows the **if** is True (i.e., nonzero), then **statement** is executed; otherwise, **statement** is ignored. When the **if-else** combination is used, **statement 1** is executed if **exp** is True, and **statement 2** is ignored. If **exp** is not True, **statement 1** is ignored, and **statement 2** is executed. Notice the following:

```
if(fd = = ERROR)                       if((c = getchar()) != '\n')
     put("Can't open file");              putchar(c);
                                       else
                                            putchar(CLEARS);
```

In the first example, if variable **fd** equals the symbolic constant for **ERROR**, the message is displayed. The expression in an **if** statement often uses a relational operator. The second example also tests for inequality between **c** and a newline character. If **c** is a newline character, then the screen is cleared through the **else** statement.

The **if** statement can also be used as:

```
if(ptr)
     statement;
else
     puts("Not valid pointer");
```

If a pointer contains an address of zero, it is an invalid pointer. A nonzero pointer value, however, is okay. The **if** statement above tests for a nonzero rvalue for pointer.

break

The **break** statement is used to "break out" of a controlling **for**, **while**, **do**, or **switch** statement. One way **break** is used is for leaving a loop when a specified value of a variable is found. The following is an example:

```
for (i = 0; i < MAXLOOP; ++i) {
     if (x[i] == MAXVAL)
          break;
     statement 1;
     statement 2;
}
statement 3;
```

When variable x[] is equal to MAXVAL, the break statement is executed, which causes control to proceed to statement 3. If x[] does not equal MAXVAL, statements 1 and 2 are executed, and the for loop keeps executing until x[] equals MAXVAL, or i equals MAXLOOP.

continue

The continue statement, which causes a for, do, or while loop to repeat execution, is the opposite of a break statement in that continue sustains control of the loop. Notice the example below.

```
for (i = 0; i < MAXLOOP; ++i) {
     if (x[i] == MAXVAL) {
          ++count;
          continue;
     }
     statement 1;
     statement 2;
}
statement 3;
```

In this example, if x[i] equals MAXVAL, the variable count is incremented and the continue statement causes the for loop to execute again. statements 1 and 2 are ignored. Also, continue is used to count the matches between x[] and MAXVAL and ignore statements 1 and 2 each time a match occurs.

switch, case, and default

Examine the following:

```
switch (exp1) {
case (constant exp2):
     statement;
case (constant exp3):
     statement;
          .
```

```
        default:
            statement;
    }
```

The **switch** statement uses the value of **exp1** to transfer control to one of the **case** statements for execution. The **constant expression** for each **case** must be an integer, and each constant must be unique. If the value of **exp1** does not match any of the **case constant expressions**, then the **default** is executed. The **switch** statement may be used to replace a series of **if** statements, like an ON-GOTO in BASIC. Study also the following:

```
switch (day_val) {
case 1:
    puts("Monday");
    break;
case 2:
    puts("Tuesday");
    break;
case 3:
    puts("Wednesday");
    break;
case 4:
    puts("Thursday");
    break;
case 5:
    puts("Friday");
    break;
case 6:
    puts("Saturday");
    break;
case 7:
    puts("Sunday");
    break;
default:
    puts("Invalid day of week");
    break;
}
```

In this example, the **switch** uses **day_val** to determine which **case** statement will be executed. The **break** statement transfers control to whatever statement follows the **switch**. Note that braces are not used for compound statements within a **case**.

while, do-while

Compare the following:

```
while (exp)                      do
     statement;                         statement;
                                 while (exp)
```

For both **while** and **do-while**, **statement** is executed as long as **exp** evaluates as nonzero. The difference between a **while** and a **do-while** is that **statement** may never be executed with a **while**. If **exp** evaluates to zero in a **while**, **statement** is not executed; **exp** is evaluated before **statement**. In a **do-while**, **statement** is executed, *then* **exp** is evaluated. Therefore, even if **exp** is zero on entry into a **do-while** loop, **statement** is always executed at least one time. For example,

```
i = count = 0;                   i = count = 0;
while (x[i] != BADVAL) {         do {
     ++count;                         ++count;
     ++i;                             ++i;
}                                } while (x[i] != BADVAL);
```

On the left of the example, if **x[0]** equals **BADVAL**, both **count** and **i** equal zero on leaving the **while** loop. If **x[0]** equals **BADVAL** for the **do-while** loop, both **count** and **i** equal 1 on leaving the loop. The statements following the **do** are executed at least one time.

goto

In the following example,

```
goto id;
```

the **goto** statement causes an unconditional transfer of control to the identifier that follows it. The identifier is a label in the program. Study the example below:

```
try:        puts("\nOutput to Screen or Printer (S,P): ");
            c = getchar();
            if (c != 'S' || c != 'P')
                 goto try;
```

If you enter any character other than an upper-case S or P, the **goto** statement executes and sends control to the identifying label **try**.

The program repeats the prompt and requests the entry again. The label must be followed by a colon, which is not part of the identifier label.

return

In the following,

```
return;          or          return exp;
```

once a function call is completed, the **return** statement returns control to the calling routine. A simple **return** statement without an expression returns an undefined value to the caller. A **return** followed by an expression returns the value of the expression to the caller.

If an expression is present, the data type returned is determined by the data type specified in the function declaration. See, for example, the following:

```
func1()                        double func2()
{                              {
     .                              .
     .                              .
     return (x);                    return (x);
}                              }
```

The call to **func1()** returns x as an integer because the **default** data type for a function is **int**. The call to **func2()** returns x as a **double** because the function is declared to be a **double**.

If a function with no **return** statement in it is called, an undefined value is returned to the caller. Program control "falls off" the end of the function, and the closing brace causes control to return to the caller.

sizeof

In the following,

```
sizeof (exp)
```

the **sizeof** statement returns an integer value that equals the size of **expression** in bytes. Take, for example,

```
y = sizeof (x);
```

```
if (y == 4)
    puts("x is a float");
```

If **sizeof** is used with an array, it determines the array size in bytes.

Macro Preprocessor and Control Lines

C has a number of control line commands that cause the compiler to include files, do macro substitutions, and do conditional compilations. For example,

```
#include "stdio.h"
#define CLEARS 12
```

tells the compiler to include the standard I/O file in the program and define **CLEARS** (e.g., a clear screen code) to be 12. Control line codes are introduced with a **#** sign and are *not* terminated with a semicolon. A newline character in the source code file signals the end of the control line. (If a **#define** is sufficiently long to warrant continuation on the next line, the backslash [\] may be used to continue the definition.)

#undef

If an identifier has been **#define**d in a program, such as **#define MAXVAL 200**, the preprocessor substitutes the value of 200 at every point in the program where **MAXVAL** appears. However, if the control line

```
#undef MAXVAL
```

appears in the program, **MAXVAL** becomes undefined from that point on.

#if

Control lines can also be used to alter compilation, depending on specified conditions. Examine the following:

```
#ifdef CLEARS
    putchar(CLEARS);
#else
```

```
        for (i = 0; i < 24; ++i)
                putchar('\n');
    #endif
```

If the symbolic constant **CLEARS** is defined (e.g., **#define CLEARS 12**) at this point in the program, the **putchar(CLEARS)** code is compiled. If **CLEARS** has not been defined, the **for**-loop code is compiled. The **#endif** marks the end of the conditional compilation.

The same results could be achieved with

```
    #ifndef CLEARS
        for (i = 0; i < 24; ++i)
                putchar('\n');
    #endif
```

If **CLEARS** has not been defined, the compiler will include the code between the **#ifndef** and the **#endif**.

Finally, an **#if** can be used to include or exclude a section of code, depending on the evaluation of a constant expression. For example,

```
    #if MAXVAL < 80
        puts("\nMaximum value is less than 80.");
    #endif
```

If the constant expression evaluates nonzero, then the code for the message is included in the program; otherwise, it is ignored.

Parametized Macros

If a program has the control line

```
    #define MAXVAL 80
```

the preprocessor will substitute the value 80 wherever it finds **MAXVAL** in the program. Let's suppose that a program has the following control line:

```
    #define sqr(X) (X*X)
```

In this case, we have a macro substitution involving a parameter that is passed to the square function.

Note what macro substitution does: at any point in the program where the **sqr( )** function is used, the compiler will substitute the square root code. In other words, there is no function call to **sqr( )**. Because "in-line" code is faster than a function call, program speed is increased. The price of this increased speed is increased memory requirements for the program because the **sqr( )** code is duplicated with each use of **sqr( )**.

When you use macros, make sure that there is no space between the name of the macro and the opening parenthesis of the argument list (if any). That is,

```
#define sqr (X) (X*X)
```

is incorrect because there is a space between the **r** and **(**.

Index

Notes

Notes

Notes

Notes

Notes

Notes